The Care and Development of the
Human Senses

The Care and Development of the
Human Senses

Rudolf Steiner's work on the significance of the senses in education

Willi Aeppli

Floris
Books

Translated by Valerie Freilich
Revised by Howard Copland and Donna Simmons

First published in German as *Sinnesorganismus – Sinnesverlust –
Sinnespflege* by Verlag Freies Geistesleben, Stuttgart in 1955
First published in English by Steiner Waldorf Schools Fellowship
Publications, London in 1993
Fourth edition published in 2013 by Floris Books in
association with the Steiner Waldorf Schools Fellowship
Third printing 2021
© 1996 Verlag Freies Geistesleben, GmbH
English version © 1993, 2013 Steiner Waldorf Schools
Fellowship Publications
www.steinerwaldorf.org.uk

British Library CIP Data available
ISBN 978-086315-987-9
Printed and bound in Great Britain by Bell & Bain, Ltd

Floris Books supports sustainable forest management
by printing this book on materials made from wood that
comes from responsible sources and reclaimed material

Contents

Publisher's note

There are many references to the teacher and to children in this book. For simplicity the author has referred to the teacher as 'he' throughout, but of course the teacher could be any gender.

Preface

Rudolf Steiner did not give us a comprehensive presentation of the senses, but he spoke about the nature and function of the sense organism of the human being in a large number of books and lectures, sometimes at length but more often only in allusions.

These statements were brought from various points of view and in various connections. Most of them contain valuable suggestions for the teacher and prove to be fruitful and enlivening for his work. They often give a new and surprising insight into the nature of education. It becomes increasingly evident that a true and comprehensive study of the senses is more necessary than ever, especially for the educator, and that such a study helps him to understand and overcome the educational difficulties arising in our time.

This book is an attempt to present Steiner's statements about the twelve human senses contained in the various books and lectures, and their importance for education. Any attempt is a venture. I am quite conscious that all his statements are of a fragmentary character, that everywhere gaps can be pointed out, and that the statements are often one-sided. In no way did I strive for completeness, which would have been quite impossible. The fundamental description in Hans Erhard Lauer's book on the twelve senses contains, as its subtitle indicates, the 'outline of a new, complete and systematic study of the senses, based on Steiner's spiritual investigations'. Lauer's work shows quite distinctly and with all the necessary foundation the epoch-making reform which has been given to our present age in Steiner's study of the senses.

The present little book is aimed in the first place at teachers and parents, but at the same time it is directed to all those people who interest themselves in the education of children and feel responsible for it.

Willi Aeppli

1. Introduction

1.1 A general conception of the sense organism

It is an easily recognizable fact that our consciousness of our self stands in closest connection with our sense perceptions. We close, as it were, our day consciousness, when we go to sleep. And alternatively the urge to sleep can become strong if no sense impressions reach us. Consequently we gain consciousness of self in the sense of ordinary day-consciousness through opening our sense organs to our surroundings. Rudolf Steiner says that, 'I-consciousness is present to the extent reached by sensory content, and sensory content extends to the extent, at least for ordinary life, that I-consciousness is present.'

Behind the ordinary experience of the I, there governs the real I of the human being. And this I, which possesses a will nature moves, as Steiner says, in the 'circumference of the twelve senses, as the sun moves in the circumferences of the twelve constellations.'[1]

There is certainly no need to demonstrate to what extent our entire soul-life is dependent upon sense impressions. There are numerous personal experiences which testify to this: how darkness evokes in us the feeling of fear and anxiety, and how quickly this mood alters when brightness enters; how our feeling is stimulated by the scent of roses, and how it is repulsed by bad smells! All sense perceptions call up feelings.

That the sense impressions work into the physical body, directly as well as through the feeling, is certainly a generally known fact, but the consequences are far too little considered, especially with regard to educational activity.

A sense perception may frighten us: we grow pale and our breathing stops. Another sense perception stimulates joyful excitement. We blush and our breathing is accelerated. In both cases a sense impression has worked on our blood circulation and our breathing.

Research has established that blind people need more vitamins and trace elements because they are deprived of light and colour stimuli, which, via the eye, very much participate in regulating and maintaining the metabolism.

And as another example a newspaper reported that a German precision tool manufacturer renovated two big workrooms. As an experiment, one workroom was painted in colours following detailed theories and experiences of colour psychology. Another room was simply decorated in the usual white and light grey. In both rooms, which were similar in every way except in the use of colour, 150 women were occupied with the same kind of work soldering, drilling, wiring, mounting, and so on. After three months the results and states of health of both working groups were compared. The result was that the women in the coloured room produced on average about 15% more than those in the other room. Sickness and absenteeism were also approximately 30% lower.

It is more than just a figure of speech to say that the

sense impressions are a kind of nutrition. A nourishment of the finest and subtlest kind takes place. Here we are no longer dealing with quantifiable substances as in our food, but with imponderable formative forces which, through the senses are able to influence the organism. However, we need to recognize that sense perceptions and the sense processes connected with them can be of significance for our health and preservation of our body.

An important educational problem immediately appears. As we know, there are suitable nourishing, wholesome foods, but there are also inferior, worthless, even spoilt foodstuffs. Could one perhaps say something similar of the sense impressions? To close this section a word from Steiner may be appropriate here:

> We possess our senses in order to perceive
> the world, to enrich the kernel of our being
> through them and to transform them to a higher
> degree of perfection ...
> Man has become the sense being which he is
> within the physical world, in order to be able to
> enrich his inner being through that which he
> absorbs through the impressions of the physical
> senses, through smell, taste, sight, and so on. All
> this is incorporated in his inner being, so that he
> possesses it and is able to use it for the further
> development of the whole cosmos.[2]

The significance of the sense organism could not be expressed more impressively than Steiner has done here.

1.2 Perception and thinking

It would go beyond the scope and task of this book to give a description of Steiner's theory of knowledge that can be found in the relevant works.[3]

However, we should look at some of the fundamentals concerning the process of cognition because this knowledge is essential to an understanding of the senses. It is important to understand how knowledge as such arises. We have first to direct our own cognizing activity to the process of cognition itself. The strange thing is that in an adult this process is not a unity but falls into two different elements: perception and thinking. We have consequently two different kinds of cognition. Let us look at the relationship of these two processes as well as on the whole process of cognition.

We face our surrounding world as human beings with a consciousness of our self. This world meets us as a differentiated world of sounds, colours, smells, forms, temperatures, and so on. We perceive these things through our sense organs.

As soon as any sense is affected by the outside world it begins to be active. As mere sense-beings we can only perceive disconnected details; here sounds, there colours, movements, and so on. Our senses as such could not establish the connections between these single perceptions. But with each perception, the second element of cognition is stirred, namely our reason, ordering the chaotic world of perception in a thinking and classifying way. Our thinking power is ready to unfold its activity whenever the opportunity arises. And such opportunities are the objects of the surrounding world, perceived by the senses. When our thinking apprehends objects perceived by the senses, concepts arise. We see, for instance, a tree; our thinking is stimulated by it and forms the concept 'tree', a conceptual counterpart to the percept. Naturally we have formed this concept innumerable times; it is at our disposal and need not be formulated anew each time. Our need to understand is only satisfied when we can develop from within – that is out of our thinking – the concept relating to the percept from without.

Only then are we certain of having grasped something of the reality of the world. What the senses bring us gives us only the one half of reality; we have to add the other, the world of concepts, ourselves. The concepts gained in this way remain in us, even when the percepts themselves are no longer there. They combine to form a system of concepts which builds the foundation of our picture of the world. We can see that cognition flows to us from two different sides, from perceiving and from thinking.

The situation for the adult of our present age is such that there is a kind of boundary between the things outside and the thoughts within. It is conditioned by our consciousness of self. It is different with small children, as will be explained in greater detail in a later chapter. With children perception and thinking lie closer together and remain more closely related, as both are nearer their common origin. So children have not yet separated themselves as much from the world as have adults. Children do not as yet face the surrounding world as something outside themselves. There is no need yet to unite through thinking what, for adults, are two strictly separated worlds – the world outside and the one within. What is not separate does not need be brought together again. That perception and thinking do not yet go such separated ways in small children is connected with the fact that they have not yet developed a consciousness of self. However, as this consciousness develops they begin to feel themselves separate from the surrounding world and experience the need to recapture through their thinking what is lost, namely the direct contact with the surrounding world which they had as small children.

In contrast to children, let us look at the higher animals and how they perceive and orientate themselves in the world. There is a saying by Goethe, 'The animal learns from its organs.' It behaves in its environment as its body, full of wisdom, determines. With human beings it is just the opposite way round: they are not from birth determined by their organs, nor do the organs enable them to relate to the world. As the consciousness of the self grows, human beings can instruct the organs and develop them to become a useful and willing instrument.

The sense organism provides the animal with perceptions and instructs it, and with each species one specific sense dominates and determines the behaviour of the animal to a great extent. When a dog pokes its nose into something, the nose only perceives the one-sided limited sensation of his organ of smell. The nose is for the dog a far-reaching organ of cognition, even if the dog is not able to comprehend the results of its investigations in concepts. But these investigations through its organ of smell are intense and achieve an abundance of canine knowledge. We can say that with the dog, smelling and thinking still form a united whole. Steiner says,

When an animal looks at something, the eye
already thinks; with man it only looks, and he
thinks with his brain. With the animal the brain
is small and imperfect. The animal already thinks
within its eye.[4]

Regarding thinking, animals do not form concepts,
as man does on the basis of sense experiences, but
already at birth carry inborn instincts. Each animal
species has its own inborn set of concepts, and the
animal can only knowingly perceive what is embodied
within it.

With human beings the senses analyse the surrounding world. Through each individual sense I
experience only one limited part of my surroundings: through the eye, the world of colour; through
the sense of warmth the differentiations of warmth;
and so on. Each sense organ is related in a one-sided
way to the world; one could say, each sense gives us
information about one part of the world. But thinking works in the opposite direction, uniting what
the seperate sense impressions have given us into a
unity of experience. Thus thinking is an activity of
synthesis. Human beings are not satisfied until what
appears separate is united. They relate the separate
sense perceptions to one another in an activity calling
on reason or judgment.[5]

Imagine a man playing the violin standing before
us. With this perception eye, ear, sense of movement,
and sense for the I of another are all active. We bring
the movements of the arm, the fingers, the violin
bow and the strings in relation to the sounds and
to the facial expressions. And if I bring these sense
impressions into relation with my thinking, I bring

order into the chaos of the sense-perceptible world, then I am in the position to reason or judge, 'This is a human being playing the violin.'

So through our twelve senses we possess a twelvefold relationship to the world and therewith an abundance of possibilities to reunite what was separated.

To which of the three activities of soul – thinking, feeling or will – is sense perception most related? Steiner often mentioned that the relation to the surrounding world through the senses, is of a will nature with a 'touch of feeling'. The will lives in the sense processes when they are functioning in a healthy way. But there is a group of senses that, notwithstanding their general character of will, nevertheless tend strongly towards cognition, and therefore may be designated as 'cognitive senses'. Similarly, there is a second group of senses, which because of their strong feeling emphasis can be spoken of as 'feeling senses'.

The reason why it is so difficult for us to be able to penetrate with our consciousness into the activities of our senses, is that they lie in our will and our feelings, and in these areas we are unconscious or only semi-conscious. In children the will character of the sense processes is especially pronounced, but as they grow up, there is a shift towards the cognitive.

Regarding misperceptions, we can ask ourselves where the error lies: in our thinking or in our per-ception? If we translate freely the Latin saying, *Errare humanum est,* with 'the possibility to err is a thoroughly human affair,' we wish to point to the positive side of the possibility to err, because the possibility of making a mistake includes the possibility of finding the truth. Animals stand beyond good and evil, and outside of error and truth. They cannot err with their perfect organism, but they do not possess the consciousness to recognize and to prove the truth. Only the human being has that possibility. We can speak of error and truth only with regard to the three logical capacities of forming representations, making judgments and drawing conclusions. It is not possible to err in the same way when perceiving through the senses, provided that the sense organs are healthy.

Goethe quite decidedly resisted the idea that pure perception could be subject to error. He could only see the possibility and danger of error in the 'combining' intellect.

> Man is sufficiently equipped for all true, earthly requirements if he trusts his senses and develops them in such a manner that they remain worthy of this confidence …
>
> The senses do not deceive, but judgment does …
>
> You may then trust the senses.
> They show you no untruth,
> If your reason keeps you 'awake'.[6]

And we can add a word by Steiner, 'The deceptions of the senses only become real errors through the intellect.'[7]

Let us conclude with an example regarding misperceptions. The sense of warmth gives us reliable information about *differentiations* of warmth. It does not indicate an absolute degree of warmth like a thermometer. In many books on physics the following experiment is described as an example of misperception.

There are three bowls, the first filled with hot water,

the second with cold and the third with lukewarm water. We put one hand into the cold, the other hand into the hot water. After a while we place both hands into the lukewarm water. The sense of warmth in the one hand now tells us, that this water is warmer compared to the water which I perceived before. But the sense of warmth in the other hand states that that this lukewarm water is considerably colder than the water tested previously.

The actual ability of the sense of warmth is to perceive *differentiations* of warmth, and this it has done accurately. So it not a misperception, but an error in reasoning not to distinguish the difference in warmth from the absolute temperature measured by thermometer.

1.3 The threefold nature of the human organism

Everything that Steiner wrote or said about the sense organism of man arose from his investigations into the entire human being. The teaching about the senses is therefore only one part of the study of the human being. One of the conditions for understanding Steiner's teachings on the senses is a grasp of the fundamental elements of the human being, as he presented on the basis of his spiritual investigations. We shall briefly describe the threefold human organism, one of the most fundamental of Steiner's discoveries. If we consider the human body we can recognize that this unity can be seen in three parts.

One part relates to the outer world through the senses at the periphery of the human organism, working its way inwards through the nerves to their central organ, the brain. The sense-nervous organization forms a homogeneous system in the entire human organism. We can speak of a 'nerve-sense human being' to characterize this part of the physical organism. This nerve-sense human being, although extending through the entire physical body, right into the fingers and toes, has its main focus in the head.

A second part of the human body is formed by the rhythmic organization: everything that is connected with breathing and blood circulation. This twofold rhythmic activity, together with the organs related to it, forms the second system. The centre of its activity, the heart and lungs, lies in the chest. We sometimes refer to this part as the rhythmic human being.

The third system encompasses everything related to metabolic activity. This takes place in all parts of the body, but mainly in the limbs. So Steiner speaks of a 'metabolic-limb human being'.

> And if you simply consider the threefold human being with regard to its activity, that is to say the nerve-senses, the rhythmical activities, and the metabolic system, then you have everything that exists in human nature, inasmuch as it is an active organism. And you have at the same time pointed out three independent systems of the human organism.[8]

Our body as a whole is the physical foundation of our soul life. So how does the soul life relate to the three parts of the body? The soul life expresses itself in a threefold way, as thinking, feeling and will. And each of these three soul forces is connected with one of the three parts of the body. It is fairly self-evident that our activity of thinking is connected with our nerve-sense system. The foundation of feeling is not situated in the nerve-sense system, but in the rhythmic system: our breathing and our blood circulation are intimately connected to our feelings. Everything connected with the will stands in closest relationships to our metabolism and limbs.

Seen from yet another point of view, we again find a threefold aspect. During the course of the day we pass through three stages of consciousness, clearly distinguished from one another. First we have the waking condition familiar to all of us. In contrast to this is deep dreamless sleep, actually a condition of unconsciousness. In between lies the state of consciousness of dreaming. So we can distinguish three states of consciousness: waking, dreaming, sleeping.

We can relate these three kinds of consciousness to the threefold physical organism of the human being. We are fully conscious and awake strictly speaking only in our thinking. We are far less aware of our will; it is much more elusive and in a certain sense we are unaware of it in the same way as when we are asleep.

In our feelings, however, we have the same state of half-consciousness as when dreaming. We therefore not only experience three successive stages of consciousness within twenty-four hours; but during the day, in our normal waking state, we live simultaneously in all three qualities of consciousness. We are *awake* with regard to our life of thinking, which is bound up with our nerve-sense system. We are *dreaming* regarding our life of feeling, which is centred in breathing and blood circulation. And we are *sleeping* with regard to our life of will, which has its organic foundation in the system of the metabolism and limbs.

2. The Human Sense Organism

2.1 The origin of the sense organs

Imagine that we live in a world which is not different from the one we are used to, that is, the world with its colours, smells, tastes; differentiations of warmth, movement, softness and hardness, and so on, but with one exception: we have to live in a world absolutely void of sound. In this case, would we possess an organ of hearing? Naturally this sense organ would be lost. The basic facts for the loss of this sense organ, however, would not be so self-evident and unequivocal. We could be easily inclined to use the 'principle of utility' as an attempt at an explanation. Goethe vehemently turned against this utility principle as a method for research. 'Why has the ox its horns? So that it can protect itself' – an example which Goethe often used to demonstrate the fruitlessness of such utilitarian explanations.

In this case the only fruitful question according to Goethe would be: what kind of formative forces are here at work to bring forth such a formation as the horn? For Goethe the questions of 'why' and 'what for' were not the questions which would lead to further understanding. Rather he sought answers to questions of the 'wherefrom', insight into the hidden formative forces which have brought forth this and that in the sense world. With regard to the problem of the non-existence of an organ of hearing in a world completely void of sound, the ear would not fall away because hearing would be useless, but because those creative forces which are at work behind the sound and which form the organ of hearing would be absent.

Something similar could be said of all the sense organs. In a world of absolute dark, no eye could develop because the organic formative forces working behind the light would not be present. Goethe expresses such facts, amongst other things, with the following words: 'The eye owes its existence to the light. Out of unimportant auxiliary animal organs the light calls forth an organ, which is to become its counterpart, and in this way the eye is created from the light for the light, so that the inner light meets the outer.'

Let us add to this a few words of Steiner's:

> How have our physical organs developed?
> Through the fact that outer forces have worked
> on them; the forces of the sun, the forces of
> sound. In this way the eye and the ear were
> created out of neutral dull organs, which to begin
> with did not allow the sense world to enter and
> which only slowly opened.[1]

2.2 Number and grouping of the senses

We are here not concerned with a sense physiology as is generally accepted. For instance, when we consider the sense of seeing or hearing, we forgo an anatomical description of eye and ear. What concerns the writer is initially to give as exactly as possible a clear presentation of the functions of these senses, as it results from anthroposophy.

The usual way to approach the organization of the senses is what I like to call the anatomical approach. The human body is investigated for sense organs in order to establish how many such organs the human being possesses. From this the quite understandable conclusion is drawn that the human being has as many sense organs as can be established anatomically. The question of whether sense organs could exist which are not so easily found but nevertheless exist has only come up in the past decades.

We mentioned previously the manifold way our surrounding world is organized, supplying us with an unlimited number of sense impressions. Is it possible to group these confused, 'chaotic' impressions? Such a consideration produces three great realms of experience, which we can call the 'surrounding world' and which the sense organs must be ready to perceive.

The first, and most obvious area of experience is that which lies outside us, namely everything of a mineral, plant and animal nature as well as our experience of other human beings inasmuch as they are beings of nature. Usually, consideration of the senses begins and ends with these realms of nature. But a more comprehensive method of observation must recognize two more worlds of perception along with their corresponding senses. These are our perceptions which lie within our own bodies; and our perceptions of the humanness of other human beings.

The former can be understood when we consider, for example, the sense of balance. And the latter becomes comprehensible when we experience our follow human beings not merely as beings of nature, but as beings of soul and spirit. In order to have such perceptions we must possess sense organs for these expressions of what is specifically human around us. And thus our entire surroundings are divided into these three realms of experience:

Our own body
Outer nature
Our fellow human beings

Steiner's work on the senses shows that for each of these realms of experience a group of four senses are involved, so that the human sense organism comprises twelve individual sense organs. The fact that we can speak of twelve senses originates neither by mere chance nor by an arbitrary theory, but is derived from insight into the nature of the human being. But now Steiner's work on the senses directs our attention upon the human being himself and shows how these groupings are also anchored in the threefold human organism.

Thus we can consider the human being as a threefold being, the following therefore can be said about the grouping of the sense organism. First we have a group of senses which stand in the closest connection to the human system of metabolism and limbs, and to the will bound to it. In those senses we shall find a specially strong will activity, and so they can be called 'will senses'. A second group of senses is the expression of the middle, or rhythmic, human being, which simultaneously gives the organic basis for the forces of feeling. Here we are concerned with the middle, or the 'feeling senses'. A third group is connected with the thinking forces which create the conditions for the activity of cognition. They are often called by Steiner the 'cognitive senses'.

2.3 The four lower senses

Before we begin to describe the individual lower senses, let us briefly stress what these senses have in common and what unites them into a group. They are all turned inward, that is, towards our corporeality, and they perceive those processes which take place in our body. Through the gates of these four sense organs our own being opens up to our own body. The processes which this sense group perceives are of objective nature. We therefore have in our body a special world of experience with organs of perception belonging to it.

It is quite obvious that strong will activity is connected with these sense functions. We use will when walking, touching, and so on. We can recognize this most clearly with the sense for own movement, but the will works indirectly in the other senses of this group, too. Because the will lives in the unconscious part of our being we therefore 'sleep away' the perceptions of our will senses. We are unaware of the processes which we perceive.

I would like to mention for the sake of completeness that these groups of sense organs can also be found in the animals, but with regard to all the twelve senses, man and animal do not completely correspond. Let us now go on to the description of the individual senses.

The sense of life

It could be said that the sense of life is the most undefined and most general within the whole sense organization. Through it we go most deeply into our body, and experience through it our corporeal existence. It enables us to experience ourselves with regard to our living corporeality within our complete inner being. The existence of this sense is specially noticed when something is perceived that is not right in our body. This sense is, for instance, noticeably active for us if we have eaten too much, drunk beyond a reasonable measure, or have slept badly. On the basis of the perceptions of our sense of life, we then can say that I am tired, hungry, thirsty; likewise that I feel refreshed, rested, satisfied. Maybe one morning we suffer from a depression, contrary to our usual temperament, and when outer circumstances for this do not exist. But the true cause could, for instance, lie in the sense of life perceiving something harmful in the liver. All soul-disturbances which have their cause in disturbed organic processes have a connection with the functions of the sense of life. It is obvious that this sense organ plays an important part in the child.

Our body's sense of time, its biorhythms, is probably connected to the sense of life. If we want to know where the actual sense organ for the sense of life is to be found, we can look toward all the physical organs of the body, such as the liver, spleen, heart and so on. Indeed, it can be said that the entire human organism is one great sense organ which functions as a sense of life.

The sense of balance, or of orientation

This sense organ gives us the possibility to rightly relate to space without losing our balance. It tells us how we have to relate to left and right, to front and behind, above and below, without falling over. I stretch out my arm, giving occasion to lose my balance, but this balance is immediately restored thanks to the 'vigilance' of the sense of balance. As long as this sense organ functions in a healthy way, I never need to lose my balance in spite of all movements. If it should cease to function for only for a moment, I would fall immediately from the chair on which I am sitting!

Steiner calls the organ for the perception of the connections between the centre of the earth and our own body, the sense for orientation. In a certain sense this 'eye' is constantly directed towards the centre of the earth. According to this, fainting would mean that the sense of balance has 'become blind' and can no longer look to the centre of the earth.

Within this group of sense organs the sense of balance occupies a special place, for it is the only sense for which a localized organ can be established, the three semicircular canals in the ear, filled with fluid, which relate to each other in the three dimensions of space. With each change of the bodily position, the fluid in these canals shifts too.

An injury to this organ reduces the capacity to maintain balance, or even extinguishes it completely. It is known that with the lower animals there are in the place of the three semicircular canals little ear-stones, and that with the removal of these organs the animal in question is no longer able to orientate in space or to move sensibly. Circus performers, acrobats, jugglers have a most finely developed sense of balance. The following comments by Steiner may be of interest to the reader:

A mathematician does not need a special construction of the brain, as many people believe. Thinking and logic works with him as with other people. What matters are those three semicircular canals situated in the ear, which are so placed to one another that they occupy the three directions of space. The special development of these organs condition mathematical talent – in this lies the ability for mathematics. It is a physical organ, and this has to be inherited.[2]

The sense of touch

Strictly speaking, with this sense organ we only perceive ourselves, our own body as with the other lower senses. Here we have to rectify a possible error as it could be asked: with my sense of touch I surely perceive the roughness of a wall, the softness of fur, the smoothness of a windowpane. In other words, I experience the outer world, but nothing of my inner self. One must reply to such a possible objection that in touching anything we certainly deal with the will coming to terms with outer surroundings. But if I touch an object, primarily I perceive only myself, that is, my own body. I perceive only the change that is called forth in myself, through the object, for instance in my fingertips, and nothing else. In touching therefore we are really concerned with processes which do not take place outside, but underneath our skin, and which we can perceive with our sense of touch.

What I perceive in this way through the organs of touch I then project with my consciousness on to the outer world and pronounce the judgment: what I touch is a rough wall. The experience of touch is in reality nothing but the reaction if our own inner being to an outer process. The outer world is being touched but nothing of its being is perceived. 'Judgment' and 'conclusion' therefore play a significant part in the activity of the sense of touch.

It is the same with the eye, with the sense of sight. I believe myself able to observe the process of touching but what I am seeing is how the fingertips move over a surface. We seem to be more familiar with this sense than with the other will senses. But here we still deal with an error because what actually takes place now is hidden from the eyes. On the other hand, there are two senses near to the sense of touch which are always taking part in its activity. If we want to find out anything by touching we move our hand or finger involuntarily. Only through movement can we gain knowledge of the outer world by touch. This fact shows us clearly the strong participation of the sense of movement in touching. Sometimes we even close our eyes when touching in order to have a still stronger experience of touch. And the sense of balance also takes part in this activity. For example, when we touch the ground with our feet we simultaneously adjust our balance.

The sense for our own movement

This sense organ tells us whether we are at rest or in movement, whether our arm is outstretched or is bent. We move a leg and perceive this movement, even with closed eyes. The change with regard to position and place of the individual members of the body whilst moving is consequently perceived through this organ. It gives us an experience of a special kind regarding our physical existence. The sense of movement 'works' very precisely. Normally movements of as little as an angle of 0.038 degrees are perceived, for example when turning the elbow joints. This sense perceives the very finest movements which take place in our body! It is also this sense which reveals most clearly the character of the will. Every movement which we perform with our body is a visible expression of our will.

Steiner called this organ of perception 'sense of our own movement', as if he wished to emphasize that with this sense we can only perceive the process of our *own* movement. Thus a question with potent consequences is put before us: what about movement outside ourselves? I surely 'see' another person who moves, the animals which move, the car which races along. With my eyes alone I can certainly not perceive them. With my eyes I can see colours and grades of shades, but not movement as such. The eye, regarding the processes of movement, is an auxiliary organ, not the primary organ of perception. Where then are the causes that enable me to experience outer movements with my own sense of movement?

The solution of the riddle lies in the fact that for most of the time we copy and reproduce all the movements outside us as soon as they move into our field of vision. This happens in a fine, most delicate manner and we are not conscious of it. In a crude way this happens, for example, with the head, if we gaze after a moving vehicle, or with the muscles of our eye, if we observe a circular movement. This most delicate sympathetic vibration of our body is perceived by our own sense of movement and is then related by our consciousness to the surroundings. We are with our own apparatus of movement, with our entire system of muscles, a member moving along with our surrounding, moving world. So we have to consider that in reality there does not exist in any place of our body a muscle moving in a completely isolated way. Steiner says that, 'even the smallest movement we make is not only localized in a part of our muscle and movement system, but arises out of the whole human organism of movement.'[3]

Sight and sense of movement, although two senses functioning in quite different ways, work very closely together. Steiner demonstrated this by using the experience of a red, circular surface.[4] Through a separate activity of the eye we would only perceive the red on the white background. But we owe to the sense of our own movement the fact that we can run along the boundary between red and white, and in this way perceive the circular line. With my sense of sight I can just as little perceive the circular form as I can sense colours with my sense of movement. We are dealing here with an extremely intimate joint play of these two senses. There is no actual seeing without the sympathetic movement of our muscles, which means without the activity of our sense of movement. Steiner explains:

> The sense of movement pours forth into
> the eye ... The form of the circle you see in
> using unconsciously the sense of movement.
> Consequently you fetch the form out of
> your entire body, in appealing to the sense of
> movement, which is spread over the whole
> body.'

In order to perceive forms which belong to the field of experience of the lower senses, I need the assistance of the eye. If I am blind, I must sense the forms through touch. The example of the coloured circular surface points us to another important fact. It is clear that my sense of movement is active if I actually run a circle with my legs or draw one with my hands. But even when another person runs a circle or draws such a geometrical figure in front of my eyes, it should not be difficult to imagine, on the basis of the previous example, the functioning of the sense of movement. The example which Steiner brought to our attention concerns a circular shape whose formation I have not been engaged with. The circle has already come to rest, has become static. Nevertheless I am stimulated to reconstruct it inwardly, to run along its boundaries. I change the circle through my own activity into something mobile. In the same way in which all geometrical figures are movement having come to rest, I am in the position to change them back again into movement.

Now our whole environment consists to a great extent of such form elements as circle, straight line, curve, triangle, square and so on. In other words, every form, every line, everything of extension length, width, depth, all the surfaces and corners of a body we perceive with our will senses, mostly with our senses of balance and of movement.

We can still go further and say that everything, which can be determined in our surroundings by number, measure and weight belongs within the experienceof the four will senses. This is so for everything that belongs to the realm of mathematics and geometry. Both disciplines of knowledge are founded upon the perception of the will senses raised to the level of consciousness. And of course our whole modern world with all its technology is built upon mathematics and geometry.

2. THE HUMAN SENSE ORGANISM

2.4 The four middle senses

Here we are concerned with those senses that gather the sense impressions that outer nature offers us. Let us assume that we are sitting at the edge of a wood on a warm summer day. In the sun it is hot, but in the shade cool. We feel the warmth here, the coolness there. We see the blue of the sky, the white of the clouds, the variegated colours of the butterflies. We smell the scented hay in the field or the resin which flows from the tree trunks. We may taste the red strawberries and experience their sweetness. Which are the senses that provide such a situation, that we can be so closely connected to nature? Certainly the following four:

The sense of sight
The sense of smell
The sense of taste
The sense of warmth

Later we shall explain why we do not count hearing in this group of senses.

Of these four sense organs we can quite generally say that they bring us messages from outer nature. Three of those have been known since Aristotle. They belong to the traditional senses, whose organs are anatomically easily demonstrated. The sense of warmth, however, is an exception; we cannot establish a localised organ for it. There was a time when the sense of warmth was joined together with the sense of touch, because they have a certain similarity with one another.

We can also say of this group of senses that they are present in the higher animals too. And it is especially characteristic of this group that they are concerned with the feeling life of the human being. Let us now turn to the presentation of the individual senses.

The sense of sight

The eye is the most dominant sense organ of present day human beings. This is one reason why it is customary to use the word 'see', instead of the word 'perceive', the latter being valid for the entire twelve senses, whereas the former, strictly speaking, has only validity for the perception of colours and graduations of shades. I 'see' a coloured circle, a horse which runs off, a cathedral, and so on.

In this connection let us mention something about colours, the content of perception of the sense of seeing. There are pigment colours which are part of the objects; the painted window-sill, the green of a leaf, the red of a rose, the yellow and black spots of a cat's fur, and so on. But there are also iridescent colours which almost hover freely, are not immediately part of the object. There are colours, which, to use an expression no longer quite unusual, are at least of a 'semi-ethereal' nature. We can think of the rainbow or the spectrum formed by a prism. Starting from such phenomena, it is no longer completely absurd to ask if, for example, a free hovering iridescent red or blue, a colour that is not tied to an object, is at all conceivable? To think that something like this is possible and acceptable, would presuppose that colours possess an objective nature.

In principle the same question can also be put when considering the sense of warmth. We speak of warmth, meaning nothing else but warm air, warm water, a hot iron, and so on, things that are permeated by warmth.

But if warmth is an independent world of experience, that can be apprehended by the senses, then there must or should exist a warmth 'in itself', a freely existing warmth which is in no way bound to another element, as for instance water, air or stone. At least this warmth must be conceivable as having an innate, independent existence.

Let us now consider after-images. We look, for example, at the flame of a candle, then we close our eyes and we see the after-image of the flame; we see how it alters by and by and finally fades away. Or we look for a time at a red spot, then look at a white paper and experience the after-image of this colour spot in the complementary colour green. We know how many experiments Goethe carried out to find the secret of these after-images. And it is known how much he resisted judging these after images only subjectively.

What has anthroposophy to say about it? The process of perception as such is comparable with the most delicate process of breathing. The latter, as is well known, consists of breathing in and breathing out. We breathe in air rich in oxygen and exhale air rich in carbon. What has been exhaled is a counterpart of what has been breathed in. A comparable process takes place when perceiving. We 'breathe in' sense impressions. We then 'exhale' them. The after-images we can consider as the exhaled sense impressions. We imprint them, according to Steiner, in the 'universal ether'. This is not only subjective but is an objective process!

It is not too difficult to demonstrate the feeling character of these four senses. Already a modest meas-ure of self-observation could enlighten us about this. It is interesting that the wisdom which lies in language points quite distinctly to the feeling character of this group of senses. If we wish to give our feelings distinct expression, we use phrases which are borrowed from the perceptions of these senses.

The sense of smell and sense of taste

This is quite striking with regard to smelling and tasting, which are indeed the most distinct feeling senses. Expressions, familiar to everyone, may be cited here:

> This is a matter of taste
> Tastefully furnished
> How tasteless!
> A boring, insipid person
> A bitter truth
> This smells fishy
> His character stinks!

The following expressions illustrate how the sense of warmth is also connected with feeling:

> A glowing admirer
> I am burning with love
> My heart grew warm
> A cool reception
> An ice-cold judgment

Even with the sense of colour we can easily experience an emphasis on feeling. Through the sense of sight we show a very slight tendency to approach cognition. If we wish to express something less of a feeling nature but more of a thinking nature, we often choose words which actually express visual perceptions.

I speak for example of insight, foresight, and hindsight. Even if we are here still slightly reminded of feeling, we are clearly aware of the thinking element. To the same extent to which the sense of sight approaches the senses of cognition, so the sense of warmth approaches the will senses. This could also be shown from the point of view of language.

Let us in addition mention the significance of the two substances of incense and perfume for our feeling life. Their use and their effects point in exactly opposite directions, the former to the religious realm, and the latter to the worldly realm.

Now let us consider some aspects of the organs of these senses. It is not the place here to speak of the complexity of the eye. Smell and taste are commonly referred to as the 'chemical' senses, and their organs are relatively simple.

The sense of smell is limited to a few niches in the upper part of the nasal cavity, into which the nerves of smell extend. The air, carrying its various scents travels through the nose. When it comes to the sense of taste, we find clearly differentiated areas on the tongue, the taste buds in each area responding to one taste, for example, to sweet, spicy, or bitter.

Other facts concern us here. Everything we taste must first be dissolved by the saliva. Therefore we cannot taste anything that has not first been changed into fluid. It is quite impossible to taste something solid. Only a small part of our physical body consists of solid substances, as for example bones, muscles and teeth. We are 'fluid beings' to a far greater extent. And this part of our bodily nature is the one which tastes, because it mixes with the fluids which come from outside.

Concerning the sense of smell and its organ, we know

that we can only smell what is of an airy nature. We are not able to smell anything solid or fluid, but only what has evaporated. We don't smell the solid rose, but what has transformed itself into a gaseous condition. That is the scent of a rose. To the same extent to which we are 'fluid human beings', we are also 'airy human beings.' It is the latter which is able to perceive the airy element, which penetrates from without. As with the fluid part of the body, like is perceived and recognised by like.

The sense of warmth

So how do we perceive warmth and cold? Where does the physical organ for the sense of warmth lie? With the sense of warmth we cannot even find such a limited sense organ as with the sense of smell. Within each of us there lives, as it were, our own organism of warmth. If we perceive cold and warmth, it is this inner warmth sense which, in a direct way, that is without an outer sense organ, perceives outer warmth. This warmth organism, which is simultaneously a sense organ, penetrates the whole body (though not uniformly). The single exception is the eye. The eye is insensitive to warmth and cold.

What creative forces work behind the organs of the middle sense group, behind the human being of fluid, of air and of warmth? Steiner describes these centres of force working behind the sense world as four distinct kinds of ether. It is the light ether, which has created the eye, the warmth ether, our sense of warmth. It is the life ether, which can be brought into connection with the power of smell, and the chemical ether with the organ of taste.

2.5 The four upper senses

Let us imagine a person in conversation with another. He listens carefully to what the other one has to say to him. We assume that at this moment he is not interested in anything else, but what his companion, through the medium of speech, wishes to express to him as thoughts about any field of knowledge. Our hypothetical listener hears the sound of the other's voice, perceives words, understands his thoughts, concepts and perceptions, and is not for a single moment uncertain about the fact that the one who speaks is, like he himself, a being imbued with an individuality, an I.

Between the speaker and the listener, regarding their attitudes, there exists at this moment a very important difference. The speaker is, in a certain selfish way, active; he develops thoughts and ideas, he shapes them into words and sentences, he lives in an active element. The attentive listener, on the other hand resigns as such his own thoughts and opinions and fashions himself in a selfless way into a pure organ of perception for thoughts which are not his own. If he would start to produce his own whilst listening, he could not perceive the thoughts of the other.

Here we have an impressive example of what Steiner has given with his teaching of on the senses. We can understand that when we are in a conversation with a fellow human being, we are dealing with real sense organs. The sound, speech, thought and I of the other person are a reality which can be perceived by us through sense organs.

The consequences of this discovery for human life in general and especially for education, cannot be disregarded. These four senses are designated by Steiner in the following way:

Sense of sound or hearing
Sense of language, word or speech
Sense of thought, concept or representation
Sense for the I of oneself and of others

What unites these senses is that they tell us about the higher nature of the other human being, because voice, language, thought are expressions of the I-endowed human being who, precisely because he is an I lifts himself out of the connections of mere laws of nature. Via this group of senses one can perceive what the creative spirit of the other human being produces and represents. These organs have the character of cognitive senses. In their perception there simultaneously vibrates an activity of cognition. Further, the sense organs, in order to function properly, presuppose that the listener can speak and develop their own thoughts. The perceiving person is presupposed to have their own sound organism and own concept organism as well as their own experience of self. This refers so far to the adult. The situation regarding the child is slightly different because, with the exception of hearing, all these senses are not yet developed in very small children.

Furthermore three of these senses (sense of language, sense of word and sense for the I of another) are not possessed by animals. They represent the specifically human element. Modern science does not recognize these senses because of their spiritual nature. For the modern way of thinking, the word, the thought, and the I are mere abstractions, which do not harbour in themselves anything of a perceptible nature. How could anyone thus suppose the existence of sense organs to perceive something which have no reality? Another factor, which makes it difficult for the investigator to get close to these senses is that, with the exception of the ear, no localized organs seem to exist for them.

Nevertheless, the activity of these higher sense organs is the prerequisite for any spiritual, and consequently real, culture for they are the basis for every social attitude within the human community. A degeneration of these organs of perception would mean at first an ever-growing isolation of one person from another, and finally, from such isolation, the war of all against all could arise. The latter therefore would presuppose the decadence of the cognitive senses. We could never develop and live to be free for our own humanity, if we did not have human beings around us imbued with a sense of self, if we never had perceived voice, word, thoughts of other similarly endowed human beings, and if we did not possess organs of perception to perceive these manifestations of the human spirit.

Let us try to describe the functions of the individual senses more exactly.

The sense of sound or hearing

Steiner mostly employs the expressions 'sense of sound' or 'hearing' when these sense organs are to relate to another person. Hearing occupies within these four sense organs a certain exceptional position. We can rightfully say that we also perceive outer nature by means of the ear, the rustling of the leaves, the twittering of the birds, the noise in the street. Therefore the sense of sound belongs just as much to the middle as to the upper senses. The fact that this sense is noticeably orientated towards the world of feeling points in this direction too. Having a Janus head, the sense of sound represents a transition from the middle to the upper senses. It looks towards nature and perceives everything that sounds out of nature, but it listens just as much, even far more intensely, towards the human being. Through the timbre of the human voice, the listener is able to understand – to recognize – that which is human in the speaker's voice. And even when this sense of sound is turned towards outer nature, it does not cease to act as a cognitive sense. It supplies us with very special knowledge about the objects of the outer world. I beat a metal plate, it begins to ring and reveals something of the substance of the metal. According to Steiner, it is the soul of the thing itself which vibrates inside and speaks to us as a sound.

In the human voice, even if it does not rise to song, there lives a musical element which is perceived with the sense of sound. Each human voice has a fundamental tone and a certain number of overtones. If the voice has too few overtones, for instance only six instead of ten, it sounds weak or ill. If there are too many, for instance fifteen, the voice sounds sharp and makes the listener restless. If the high overtones are absent, the voice sounds round and warm and thereby establishes good contact with other human beings. With our sense of sound we recognize the kind of voice of the other, and through this something of his individuality.

Further, the hearing spectrum of the adult has a compass of nearly ten octaves, each octave having twice as many vibrations as the previous one. The ear drum moves to and fro when it responds to the softest sound still perceptible to us, which is a nanometre, or a millionth part of a millimetre. If we hold one ear towards a sound, this sound takes an additional thousandth part of a second to reach the other ear.

Two questions still need to be addressed. The first: what can our ear really experience, if for instance it turns to outer nature? It can establish the strength, pitch and timbre (tone-colour) of a sound, but not the distance or direction of the same. Mistaking this fact is the cause for a number of phenomena being wrongly interpreted and thus labelled as a misperception. Perhaps we hear in the silence of night a faint noise, as if someone was walking up and down carefully in front of the house stopping now and again. We get up, ready to catch the uncanny night wanderer and discover that the reason for the noise is a butterfly, fluttering between curtain and windowpane. It is not the ear that has deceived itself, because it has perceived quite exactly pitch, strength of sound, kind of sound and its duration. It is our faulty reason which has created a fantasy and drawn the wrong conclusion.

The second question now arises and it is not unlike the question about colour and warmth. It could be formulated in the following way: It is a matter of fact that the sound we hear has a connection with the rhythmical vibrating air. But are sound and vibrating air therefore identical? Is it not conceivable that the sound has to use the rhythmically moving air as a vehicle in order to be noticed by our ear because of its structure? Is a reality hidden behind such a thought? To earlier peoples, who spoke of the music of the spheres, the freely hovering sound which does not require the medium of the air was quite conceivable.

The sense of language, word or speech

Here is a sense we do not share with animals. If, for instance, a dog understands his master, then it is certainly not by virtue of a developed sense of speech or language. The sense for language (or the word) is a specifically human sense, enabling one to understand the language of one's fellow human beings. Language, being divided into vowels and consonants, and being expressed by the words themselves, as well as by word order (syntax), represents an independent world of existence. To understand language is not merely to hear sound. What enables one to understand is the *ability* to understand, to be a cognizing being. We must not confuse this with the separate ability to hear sound.

Because, as a rule, we speak not for the sake of language itself but rather to express our thoughts and our will, we can overlook the fact of language's independent existence as a sense. A person who listens to another speaking does not listen to the language itself but generally simply wants to know the speaker's meaning, his reason for speaking. Language perceived as language itself rarely happens. Because of this and because language is terribly misused, the sense of speech is the most corrupted organ amongst the twelve senses.

To the same extent as every perception precedes a judgment, so also does perception precede language. Before the child is capable of thinking and judging in a cogent way, his developed sense of language turns to the language around him. The child consequently still retains a direct relationship to sound and word similar to our impression of colour. The adult has a sound organism enriched by the decades of experience of the sense of sound. This organism is still small in the young child, and does not yet exist in the infant. The following quotation from a lecture by Steiner may serve the widening of our conception of the sense of language:

> The perceived sound is not the only thing through which such an inwardness is revealed to the human being, as is the case with the sound of language. Also gesture, mimicry and physiognomy finally lead to something simple and direct, which belongs just as much to the realm of the sense of language as the content of the audible sound.[5]

The sense of thought, concept or representation

Through this sense organ we are in the position to unite ourselves with the concepts, representations and thoughts another person has formed. Thus I can have a direct observation of what is revealed in the concept. Of the higher senses, the sense of thought is the most distinct sense of cognition, a fact which easily misleads people to the notion that in perceiving the thoughts of others we are also concerned with our own thinking activity. But if I am a really attentive listener, one who wishes to follow the train of thoughts of the speaker, I can only do so if my attitude to the other is such that I silence my own thinking activity. There is a fundamental difference between myself and the other. If I start with my own thought activity, the possibility of perceiving someone else's concepts and representations ceases.

As a thinking being I extinguish my own thinking while listening, and put in its place the thinking of the other, taking hold of it as an experience comparable to my own. I actually have perceived the thinking of the other person. Therefore, while listening I am by no means 'thoughtless'. I put in the place of my own thinking the thinking of the other. However, at first I have to perceive this thinking of the other person. Steiner says that,

> this is experienced in my own consciousness, in that in experiencing the content of the other person's consciousness, I experience my own just as little as I experience it in my dreamless sleep. To the same extent to which, as in the latter, my day consciousness is eliminated, so is my own in perceiving the content of the other person's consciousness ...
>
> Through the sense of concept we become capable of understanding the concept in a perceptual way, which does not clothe itself in sounds of language. In order to be able to judge, we must have concepts. If the soul is to stir, it must first be able to perceive the concept. For this purpose it needs the conceptual sense, which is in the same way a sense by itself, as perhaps the sense of smell or of taste.[6]

I use language in order to express my thought. Language is for me the mediator of my thoughts, although it has its own content of perception. It is important to clearly differentiate language and thought and the two sense organs belonging to them.

To express our thoughts there are other possibilities in addition to language. There are gestures. I gesticulate, for instance, with my arms; the other person understands the thought expressed by this gesture and stops, as I intended. I ask him something, he shakes his head and through his gesture I have perceived his thought. Perhaps he has only raised his eyebrows, hardly noticeably, but I have understood his reply made with the help of eye and sense of movement. Two people, who speak different languages, can express their thoughts extensively through gestures and mimicry. We can also give expression to our thoughts by writing or by signs.

I can either answer a question by saying distinctly 'yes', or by only nodding with my head, or likewise by writing YES on a piece of paper. In all three cases my thoughts are perceived by another with the help of their sense of thought. In the first case the sense of sound and of word was used, in the second and third the sense of sight and that person's own movement. Japanese, Koreans and Chinese, although they speak different languages, have the same symbols for their concepts and representations. Although, for example, the word 'tree' is differently expressed in the three spoken languages there is for all the three people only one and the same symbol for the concept 'tree'. Consequently they can to some extent communicate their thoughts by writing, though each speaks their own language. Throughout the world international signs are used to express certain concepts, for example, numbers or traffic signs. These are understood regardless of the language spoken by the observer.

A direct perception of someone else's thoughts is not a rare experience, provided that there is an identical or very similar organism for concepts and a harmonious spiritual-soul relationship. It can happen that my partner answers a question which I had only put in silence, entirely in thoughts. This is a case where in external, ordinary life thoughts are perceived in a direct way with our sense of thought. So people perceive by means of their sense for concepts another's inwardness, external to themselves. And they add what they perceive to their own existing organism of concepts. Actually, they only perceive those concepts living in another human being that live in themselves, at least in a similar way. Two people who live in entirely different worlds of concepts, that is to say, who have entirely different organisms for concepts, will therefore find it difficult to come to an understanding in spite of the aid of their 'sense of representation.'

The sense for the I of oneself and of others

This is undoubtedly the most difficult sense to understand. One of the difficulties is that we have to recognise that the I of another person is something real, and not simply something supersensory. Even more than with the sense of thought or of language, we have to acknowledge the reality of the *content* of our perception.

To reach a better understanding we need to limit what is meant in three directions. Firstly, it is not a perception of our own self, our own I; secondly it is not a supersensory experience of an imaginative kind; and thirdly it is not simply a logical conclusion drawn from other sense perceptions. To gain a better understanding we shall quote Steiner's actual description:

Just in the same way as seeing or hearing
does not depend on a conclusion, so
perceiving someone's I does not depend on
a conclusion, but is a direct, real truth which

is gained independently of seeing the other
person or hearing his sounds. Apart from
perceiving his language, apart from seeing his
flesh colour, letting his gestures work upon
us, apart from all that, we perceive directly
the I of another human being. And as little
as the sense of seeing is connected with the
sense of tone, so little is the perception of
'I' connected with the sense of sight, the
sense of tone or any other sense. It is an
independent sense for the I.
Until this is understood the science of the
senses will not rest upon solid foundations.[7]

Steiner characterises the perception of another
person's I as a very complicated process. He gives a
detailed description:

If you meet another person, the following
occurs: For a short period of time you perceive
a person, and he or she makes an impression
upon you. That impression disturbs you
inwardly; you feel that the person, a being
comparable to yourself, makes an impression
upon you like an attack. The result is that you
defend yourself inwardly, you resist this attack
and become inwardly aggressive towards the
person. In this aggression you become crippled,
and the aggression ceases. Then the other
person can again make an impression upon
you, and after you thus have time to regain
your aggressive strength, you carry out another
act of aggression. Again you become numb, and
the other person again makes an impression

upon you, and so forth. This is the relationship that exists when one person meets another and perceives the other I – that is, devotion to the other – inner resistance; sympathy – antipathy. I am not speaking now of feeling, but just the perception of meeting.[8]

In this process of meeting sympathy and antipathy play an important supporting role. When we approach another person, we unconsciously use the force of sympathy to an extent. But in order not to lose ourselves in the other person, we must again return to ourselves. This we do by using the opposite force of antipathy to an extent. However, neither force is used to excess, for if antipathy predominates we would not be able to really meet the other; if sympathy overwhelms we lose ourselves in the other – something of this happens for a time when falling in love.

The human being, perceiving with the upper senses, must first have their own I-experience, must have a certain consciousness of self, to be able to perceive with that I-sense the I of the other person. How this stands with regard to the young child will be dealt with later in the book.

2.6 The relation between the lower and upper senses

Understanding the relationship between the lower and upper senses can be quite difficult. The statements and presentations given by Steiner concerning this are not numerous, but they possess a very penetrating character. They are rich in consequences, especially for educational practice, so that it is both essential and rewarding for the educator to occupy himself intensely with this work.

We can start with the fact that the four upper senses are the actual human senses, which only human beings can call their own. We naturally all know that hearing, which also belongs to the group of the upper senses, is developed with the higher animals, often to a much higher degree. But for human beings the sense of sound has a special quality which includes the ability to perceive what comes to expression as specifically human. The animal is not capable of such perceptions, because, as a being without awareness of self, without an I, it has an organ capable of roaring, mewing, neighing, croaking, but not of producing a human voice. Starting from such observations we can ask why these sense organs could not develop in the animals. And, where do these forces work in the animal, which with man – without his own conscious participation – developed the four higher sense organs?

One answer has already been given. It is the human I force which works behind the formation of these organs. The animal, although endowed with elementary soul capacities, lacks this force of the I. With this another fact is closely connected. The animal lives so completely in its bodily nature and in its sense organism, that nothing is left for the development of the cognitive senses. The boundless vitality of the animal does not permit the formation of the upper senses.

It is just another small step to consider whether humanity's lack of such boundless vitality – an unconscious renunciation – perhaps caused the development of these cognitive senses?

The concept of metamorphosis can aid us in understanding the relationships which rule between the lower and the upper senses. If we bring ourselves to investigate metamorphosis with regard to outer nature, to partake in it in Goethe's sense, we witness everywhere and at any time the strangest and most wonderful transformations which, however incomprehensible they are to the intellect, we nevertheless have to acknowledge. Let us remember the metamorphosis which a seed goes through before it becomes a fully-grown plant; or the egg of a frog, developing through the state of the tadpole to the frog; or, to mention the most magnificent example, the caterpillar which transforms itself via the state of the chrysalis into a butterfly. Materialistic ideas do not readily explain such transformations.

Such transformations are pertinent when dealing with the hidden relations between the lower and the upper senses. Only they are not as obvious as with the above-mentioned examples. In the course of our further presentations we shall follow to a great extent the descriptions of Steiner which as far as possible we will reproduce in the original wording.

We find further insights into Steiner's teaching of the senses by asking about the *organs* of the four upper and the four lower senses. Outside anthroposophy little has been said concerning the organs of the will senses and nothing about those of the cognitive senses.

Let us start with the will senses. The organ for the *sense of our own movement* is characterized by Steiner as 'the physical organism of the capacity of movement,' or also as 'the whole physical movement apparatus'. Concerning the organ for the sense of life, we find in Steiner the following characterizations, for example, 'The liveliness working in our body ... The living agility of our entire physical organism ... Every individual physical organ is simultaneously an organ of perception of the sense of life.'[9]

The organs of the *sense of touch* are known. It would be the outline of the entire human figure, if we would connect with one another all the little corpuscles of touch. The *sense of balance* is localized in the ear. But thereby the compass of this sense organ is by no means exhausted. It would be fair to see in the statically orientated living structure of the bones, something of a great, outspread organ of the sense of balance.

If we now ask for the organs of the higher senses, then anthroposophy provides some surprises. In a certain sense we are actually directed to the same organs which form the basis of the will senses, although these two sense groups represent the greatest contrasts. But hidden relationships can be found in polarities. Steiner spoke about the organ of the *sense of thought:* 'The organ for the perception of someone else's thoughts is all that we are, inasmuch as we feel in us agility, life … the lively agility which we carry in us, in so far as it expresses itself in the physical body, is the organ of perception for the sense of thought.'[10] This sounds at first like the description of the organ for the sense of life.

About the organ of the *sense of language,* we read in the same lecture by Steiner, 'We could not understand any words if we did not have in us a movement apparatus … Our entire movement organism is sense organ for the word – perception.' Has not the same already been said about the sense organ of the sense for our own movement?

Therefore the question for us is, wherein lies the essential difference between the sense of thought and the sense of life, or the sense of language and the sense of movement? Now Steiner adds to the description of the organ of language: 'Only that we, in perceiving the words *keep* this movement organism *at rest*. It is just because we keep it at rest, that we perceive and understand the words ... I understand what the other person says through the fact that I arouse in myself the movement organism somehow only as far as my fingertips, but *restrain the movement*, keep it back, constrain it. In constricting the movement I understand what is spoken.'

Regarding the sense of thought, Steiner says: 'Coming into existence, it is immediately a transformed organ of the sense of life.' Such words contain the solution of the riddles presented here. Here a 'renunciation', not at all conscious to us is pointed to. Original intentions, which can lead to the development and strengthening of will senses, are not carried out. The forces thereby becoming free transform themselves, and can be led to other functions and bring about, from now on, the formation of higher sense organs.

In the same way in which the thought sense is the transformed sense of life, and the language sense the transformed sense of movement, so the transformation of the sense of touch results in the sense of I and the sense of balance transforms into the sense of hearing or sound.

> If the forces [which otherwise are active behind
> the will senses],before they arrive at the limits
> of their activity, are preserved by the inner
> formation processes of germinal organs, they
> create out of these organs the senses of hearing,
> of sound, and the sense of thought or concept.[11]

Hence it follows that the organ of hearing is the transformed organ of balance, the organ of language is the organ, held back in its development, of the sense for one's own movement, and the sense for thought or concepts as organ of the sense of life transformed at its formation.

> Man, to the extent to which he is the *resting human body* with the head effectively as centre, is the organ of perception for the I of another human being … We ourselves, as physical beings, are the greatest organ of perception that we possess.[12]

To sum up, we can say about that with the will senses and the cognitive senses, we are dealing with the same group of qualities of the human body, which however stand in a polar relationship to each other. The group of the upper senses can be regarded as the result of a turning upside down or a sublimation of the lower senses.

Sense for touch – sense for I
Sense for life – sense for thought
Sense for movement – sense for language
Sense for balance – sense of hearing

3. The Development of the Sense Organism

3.1 Human development

The history of humankind is the story of change of consciousness throughout the centuries and millennia. As human consciousness is closely linked with the nature of the sense organs and thereby with the nature of perceptions, it is quite possible to regard the history of humankind as a history of its change with regard to the human sense organism. We owe to Rudolf Steiner important information about the change of the human sense organism in the course of longer periods of time; we likewise owe to him an outlook into the near and also distant future. A look into the past and a view into the future give us the possibility of understanding better what is happening in the present, and what kind of tasks and responsibilities we have for the future.

The following three stages of humankind's development, seen from the point of view of the sense organism, are described here quite concisely, and are reports or quotations from Steiner. The first of these three stages of human development goes very far back into the past, to a time which is described in anthroposophy as the Old Moon development. The kind of sense perception of humankind in those days Steiner describes as follows:

> The form which the human senses have today, compared with the form in existence during the Old Moon evolution, is a far more dead one. Then the senses were far more lively organs, organs full of vigour. Consequently they were not suited to the fully conscious human life, but only to the old dreamlike clairvoyance of the Moon-man. The state of this Moon-man excluded any freedom, any free impulses of action and desire ... The senses were during the Old Moon period still more life processes. When today we see or hear, this is already a fairly dead process.[1]

In this connection Steiner said, for instance, that the sense of sight was still a kind of colour-breathing organ; and that hearing was still connected with being inwardly thrilled, with an inner vibration, so that man did not perceive sound only with his physical organ for hearing, as is the case today, but partook in the sounds with his whole body in a lively way. We therefore have to imagine that these sense organs bore the character of life processes. Life processes of present-day man are, among other things, breathing, nutrition, growth and secretion. The human being of older days who could not yet be regarded as a being imbued with an individuality, an I, possessed seven such senses functioning in a living way, which were the foundation of the dreamlike, clairvoyant consciousness. Only during the later evolution of the earth have all the twelve senses developed, and therewith created the condition for the development of consciousness of the self.

The second stage of human sense development leads us to the event in human history described in the language of the Bible, or in Christian tradition, as the Fall of Man, or the expulsion from Paradise. The Old Testament describes this event in majestic pictures, the Tempter saying to Eve: 'Your eyes will be opened ... knowing good and evil' (Gen.3:5). These words point quite distinctly to a change in the sense organism of man. The eye was, and is still today, the representative of all other sense organs. Steiner's spiritual investigations give us information about the kind of change that took place in the sense organism of man.[2]

How would human beings have perceived if this event had not taken place?

> Man would not have opened his senses to the
> outer world, he would only have perceived
> what was in his inner being. He would have
> felt: Within me is a zone which is entirely
> permeated by the effects of the macrocosm, and
> this I perceive.[3]

Consequently, in the process of seeing, human beings were not to perceive outer things, the colours outside, as is the case today. They were actually to *experience their eyes*. Human beings were to live inside the activity, within their sense processes, in which the divine spiritual will worked.

But now the etheric body withdrew from certain parts of the human body (Steiner describes the process in this way). These parts are consequently no longer

properly penetrated by it. Instead, purely physical
effects occur which are, so to speak, excluded from the
general life effects. The parts referred to here are those
where our present day sense organs have developed.

> The etheric body is somehow pushed back,
> and there are acts of individual physical nature
> in the physical body which are not penetrated
> by the etheric body in the corresponding
> manner; through this arises what we today call
> 'sensations'.[4]

For this reason the eye can be compared (at least
up to a point) with a camera – something the mind
has devised and human hands have produced. We
have here, as with the camera, a purely physical effect,
except that the back of eye is by no means forsaken
by all the life processes. In this way human ears and
eyes and all the sense organs were opened, so that an
individual could no longer could perceive in his sense
organs the effects of divine active forces, but began
to see, hear, smell and taste the outer world. Parallel
with this development of the sense organism ran the
development of the intellect in relation to the brain.
Both factors of development are inwardly deeply
connected. In the following chapter we shall also point
to another parallel, to the inner connection that exists
between the development of humankind and the
development of each modern individual.

Now regarding the development of this sense
organism, marked intermediate stages lie between
that event in the most distant past, which has so
fundamentally changed the sense organism of man,
and the present day. We are only too ready to assume

that the way of perceiving the outer world through the senses shows no essential difference between present day individuals and those of the past, such as an ancient Egyptian or ancient Indian.

What Steiner said in this connection about the perception of the ancient Indian, for example, is very interesting. The time in question lies several thousand years ago. In order to characterize the sense impressions of these people, Steiner uses the expression 'saturated perceptions'. This means that the people of that era were already able to perceive the contours of the outer sense impressions, but still possessed the capacity to see simultaneously the forces working behind, and which conjure up, the sense world.

For instance, they could perceive and experience the archetypal plant (in Goethe's use of the term) behind each individual plant as an outer sense impression which was maya. When observing an animal, for example a gazelle, they could also see along with the outer sense impression of the legs and hooves the formative forces which gave shape to them. In ancient India humanity's leaders were more concerned with teaching about outer sense impressions than with the forces working behind them. Today, understanding must move in the opposite direction.

It is a fact which can be shown that the ancient Greeks still possessed a more intense and lively sense life than people do today. We know that their colour spectrum was shifted towards the red end, to the side of the active colours. We know, for example, that they did not yet have a proper word to express blue. With the words *glaukos* and *kyanous* they described the dark hair of a human being as well as the blue stone, lapis lazuli, or the colour of a violet. They likewise could not yet distinguish between green and yellow, like colour-blind people today who cannot see blue. With the word *chlôros* they specified everything which we today call green, but also the yellow resin, the yellow honey and the blond hair of a person. The freshness of the sense perception of the ancient Greeks was caused by the fact that their entire bodily nature – compared with people of today – possessed a surplus of life forces. Consequently from this lively organism they could fill their sense organs with vitality. Their spiritualized organic life poured forth into their senses.

The transition of oriental to occidental civilization is closely connected with a change in the sense organization. When representing the entire sense organism of present day human beings, it was pointed out that a healthy activity of the four cognitive senses is the condition for a genuine culture. In his cycle *Man as a Being of Sense and of Perception* Steiner speaks about this in greater detail.

There he gives at first a slightly different grouping of the twelve senses. He divides them into the six upper senses (sense of I, sense of thought, word sense (or sense of language), sense of hearing, sense of warmth and sense of sight); and the six lower senses (sense of taste, sense of smell, sense of balance, sense of movement, sense of life and sense of touch). Thus half of the middle senses are attributed here to the upper, and half to the lower senses. At this point it may be mentioned that Steiner repeatedly grouped these twelve senses differently, always presenting them from new viewpoints. Of the six upper senses he said, 'all these senses furnish experiences which nourish the spiritual life, when there is spiritual life within the soul.' Steiner then directs the attention of his audience to the fact that these six upper senses formed the foundation of ancient oriental culture, and in contrast, western culture is essentially founded on the activity of the six lower senses.

> Just consider the attitude of science which has arisen and is trying to apply mathematics to everything. But mathematics comes from the senses of movement and of balance. Therefore even the most spiritual things discovered by modern science come from the lower man. But modern scientists work above all with the sense of touch ... in essence western culture is derived from the lower man. I must repeatedly emphasize that with such things there is no question of judgment, but of describing the historical course.[5]

In the previous chapter it was explained how the four lower senses, although directed towards the inner being, nevertheless perceive all that can be determined by number, measure and weight in the world. The extent of an object in the three dimensions of space, its weight and number, are grasped by the lower senses. And what these senses perceive, at first unconsciously, reaches our consciousness and leads to cognition and concepts. The representation of three-dimensional space, the law of gravity, the concepts of the perpendicular and the horizontal, the idea of certain numerical relations, and so on, are only the abstract concepts of what we experience purely as perceptions with our will senses, as facts of our own bodily nature. The realm from which mathematics and geometry as science arise, is the will-sense organism. These sciences have nothing subjective in them because they originate in that part of our whole being in which we ourselves are objective.

What we perceive with our lower senses has nothing to do with what we call our personality. What, for instance, we perceptually experience with our sense of balance as a quality of space within our body, is outside in the world. It is the same spatial world that presents the same laws in us and outside us. For this reason we speak of the objective value of these perceptions and the scientific disciplines of geometry and mathematics built on them. Mathematics and geometry are the basis and condition of our present western civilization.

However, the situation today is such that only what belongs to the realm of perception of the lower senses is regarded as objectively valid in the theoretical as well as in the practical field. Reality is only acknowledged in that which is determined by number, measure and weight. At the same time the objective character is denied to the realm of perception of the remaining senses. Modern science does not acknowledge reality to the perceptions of the eye, for instance, to colours, to the light. Only subjective significance is ascribed to these perceptions. Here likewise everything is reduced to mathematics, with the intention of arriving at objective validity. Light, colour and sound are reduced to mere vibrations, consequently to movements which are taken from the field of perception of the lower senses.

Regarding the experiences of the three upper senses, of word, thought and I, the modern way of thinking is even less capable of recognizing their objective character. What belongs to the upper senses, being denied any character of reality is therefore relegated from the realm of knowledge to that of belief, a contrast which contradicts human as well as universal truths. To this fact we have to add another. We could quite justifiably say, as we did with the six lower senses, that our present western civilization is founded upon the human intellect which has increasingly developed during the course of the past two thousand years up to its present greatest perfection. It is in fact the cooperation of both factors, the domination of the six lower senses and the development of the intellect, which have brought forth present-day civilization. They are connected with one another in a far deeper way than passing consideration can imagine. Indeed, one part of our brain came into being through the transformation of a sense organ, namely, the sense of smell.

> Because today this is already a result of outer anatomy and physiology, at least a well-founded hypothesis that our present thinking is actually rooted in a metamorphosis of the sense of smell, in so far as our thinking is bound to the brain – therefore not to the higher senses at all, but to a metamorphosis of our sense of smell.[6]

Steiner adds that although humanity could live with the culture of the upper senses, in the long run people cannot live in a human way with the one-sided culture of the lower senses.

3.2 Individual development

The question of the order in which the sense organs of the baby and the small child develop and begin to function is a vexed one. The answers of physiologists and psychologists, doctors and educators are manifold and contradictory. One can say with certainty that the will senses appear before the cognition senses and are noticeable at an early stage. Babies experience quite general physical comfort or discomfort according to whether they are satisfied or hungry. Their sense of life tells them this. As soon as they begin to kick with their legs, the sense for their own movement is brought into action. The sense of touch also develops very early. Only the sense of balance takes its time; of the four will senses it is the last to awaken and be active. We can observe how children after birth are as yet not fitted for the gravity of the earth, but gradually adapt themselves to the relationship of earthly existence. It takes months before they have adapted themselves to earthly spatial conditions. As soon as they begin to stand up we know that the sense of balance has awoken. With regard to this sense organ, we realize how helpless one is born into earthly existence.

In contrast to this with many animals it is often only a matter of a few hours between their being born and their being able to orientate themselves in space. But we see how the animal must develop its position of balance in a strictly fixed way; how all its movements are one-sided. This species is predestined to climbing, that species to flying or swimming. It is not possible for animals to place themselves in a free manner into space and to seek ever anew the balance out of themselves. How different with the human being! The way a human being is constituted means that no individual has the skill or specialization of the animals. One is not forced into a certain way of being. Rather, the human being is free and must gradually attain a relationship to space.

Though there is of course overlap in how the senses develop, the middle senses, generally speaking, develop next. When children begin to speak we know that a new sense organ has awakened in them, the sense of speech, which enables them to perceive their mother tongue and to learn it through imitation. But let us return in our considerations to the very early infant stage. We must not forget that the first perceptions of the baby are not so sharply defined by the individual sense spheres as is the case with the adults. The infant has a quite general perception of the world which is conveyed by the whole body. In the early years, although the individual sense organs are externally localized, they extend over much wider realms than they do later. Small children hear music, for instance, less with their ears than with their whole body, which vibrates and lives in this musical element. Tasting is not confined to the tongue, but extends beyond this to stomach, liver and spleen. The following remarks by Steiner point to a parallel development of the individual to humanity's development of the past.

It is interesting that the child in his first years, even if only dimly and in a dreamlike manner, really possesses this consciousness of an earlier humanity. He does not regard the outer world, but pays attention to what takes place within him. Children are mainly interested in their own body, they do not regard the outer world but possess just a dreamlike consciousness of being enclosed as in a sphere, which really takes in the effects of the outer world as pictures. The child really feels the skin as a kind of envelope and pays attention to what takes place within as pictures and sounds. This ceases to a great extent later.[7]

Steiner often speaks of how young children, approximately up to the fourth year, still possess a kind of general organ of perception in their etheric body. The task of this etheric body as organic force is at first to develop the physical organism with all the individual organs. With this, however, its function is not entirely used up. It serves simultaneously as an organ of perception of a special kind. What can the child perceive through it?

As an example, let us assume that as adults we witness an outburst of anger of an uncontrolled person. Perhaps we can observe how such a man stamps his feet, clenches his fist, bellows, rolls his eyes, how his face flushes, the veins on his forehead swell with anger, and so on. But what do small children see with their organs of perception? On the one hand something similar to what the adult sees, but beyond that the wild, uncontrolled soul force of this person, too. Small children thus have a supersensible experience. The Swiss philosopher Troxler (1780–1866) wrote, 'All small children are clairvoyant.' With this the fact is exactly described. We are dealing here with supersensible imaginations of which the child is capable just because the power of judgment is not yet developed. Why do we as a rule no longer remember such supersensible imaginations from our early childhood? Because they have sunk into our subconscious, since the power of memory was not yet strong enough to carry them over into the consciousness of the adult.

We forget them as we forget most of our dreams. If, however, such experiences made a particularly deep impression, or if they repeat themselves in the same manner, it can happen that they are remembered later. Such cases are more numerous than we imagine. Another question: what happens with this general organ of perception in the course of the individual's development? Does it simply disappear without leaving a trace behind? Or does it metamorphose, like all living things? If we investigate the development of this capacity, we see a surprising transformation. The capacity of perception appears round about the seventh year as imaginative thinking, or childlike fantasy. Is this thinking in pictures a kind of perceiving or an early kind of thinking? The answer can only be that it is both simultaneously: on the one hand an inner perception, on the other hand a young, lively thinking. This imaginative thinking also shows the tendency to develop further to the clarity and consciousness of the conceptual thinking of the adult. This demonstrates that our ordinary thinking shows a remarkable genesis. And so we can see that the individual's development today also corresponds to a great extent to humanity's development in the past.

In Section 1.2 we have shown how the entire process of cognition of the adult is not uniform, but divided into the two components of perception and thinking. How is it in this respect to small children? The one component, the forming of concepts and judgments, is not at all present. Therefore we can say in a certain sense, that the process of cognition is still a uniform one. Small children live in the world almost exclusively as beings of perception. They are completely sense organs. They are, with all their senses, completely open to the impressions of the surrounding world, completely exposed and unconditionally given up to them. Just because children are not yet in the position to catch and digest the sense impressions with consciousness, so can these impressions penetrate without hindrance into their organism. The saying 'the child consumes sense impressions' is meant more than just metaphorically. Children have no other choice than to incorporate the effects of the surrounding world by way of the sense organism. All perceptions call forth in children secretions of glands, and so if a child, for example, sees colours, there arises in the organism metabolic processes of some kind. It is no exaggeration to say that children build up their physical organism according to the sense impressions they receive from their surroundings.

> At an early age ... the child is more than merely
> in a symbolical sense, completely a sense organ
> ... All the impressions of the outer world work
> through the whole organism, whereas at a
> later stage in life they are only physical at the
> periphery of the sense system; they work further
> into the body only through the level of the soul.

Up to the change of teeth children are throughout the whole organism sense. Older children and adults experience sense impressions at their periphery, while inside is soul.

> The adult is so organized that the light with its
> physical effects stops in the eye and that only the
> representation of the light penetrated by feeling
> penetrates further inwards. With the young child
> every blood corpuscle as it were, is inwardly
> stirred physically by the light.[8]

Up to the time between the ninth and tenth year, the two functions, perception and thinking, have not yet separated to the extent they do later. The child still possesses the liveliness of perception caused by the enlivening etheric forces in the sense processes. These forces do not yet show the later degree of fading away. The sense impressions also still carry a distinct character of will. Such facts result in an extraordinarily lively relationship with the outer world before the tenth year. The child's thinking is likewise still fresh and young, filled with etheric life and ready at any time to bear witness of its origin from the entire sense organ. As yet the child has not the intellectual, somewhat dried out thinking, which tries to lay hold of the world in sharply outlined concepts. This imaginative thinking, which is simultaneously revealed as inner perception is still filled with the forces of life and will, like the sense organism itself. For this reason perception and thinking lie close to each other at this early stage of life.

As already mentioned, the activity of judgment is not yet born in the small child. In its place there is the absolute devotion to the surrounding world. Children whose intellectual forces are not prematurely developed answer before their tenth year to the impressions of the surrounding world with inner agility right into their organism; with awe and expressions of will, but not with concepts and abstractly determined judgments. Towards the tenth year a great change takes place. At about this time, children rightly experience the first intellectual awakening in their thinking. The living, imaginative forces carried by the will withdraw or experience a transformation. In a similar way the forces of life and will in the entire sense organization also withdraw. That which up to now united perception and thinking, namely the processes of life and will, decreases. The two functions, perception and thinking, go their own way; they separate. This process brings serious consequences for children. They experience themselves placed in a new relationship to the world, namely, facing it. They are forced to see this world with 'different eyes'. Everything appears differentiated, somewhat stranger and more questionable. The have to try to understand their perceptions with his newly won thinking and their changed sense organism. They begin to come to terms with the world. We could also say that a further epoch of expulsion from Paradise is reached. Such changes in the child's sense organism and thinking-organism have to be taken into account by the educator and borne in mind in teaching.

The loss of the sense organism

The present sense organism of humankind has passed through a long history of development. Only a little of this could be indicated here, but this brief description was necessary in order to understand the future development of the senses. Few people would doubt that this sense organism can remain for ever in its present stage of development; it will change in the future in one or another direction. We are faced with the question as to which direction this change will take. Humankind is today standing at a crossroads. There are many distinct signs that, owing to the conditions of our present time, our sense organism is being driven into decline, unless a new reviving influence emerges.

The senses are endangered from two sides, from purely intellectual abstract thinking and from modern civilization with all its technical achievements.

The connection of these two factors is obvious. We carry in our consciousness too little of the connection which exists between, on the one hand, the brain and nervous system upon which our thinking rests, and on the other hand, the sense processes. In Section 1.2 it was shown how perception and thinking are subordinated to the entire function of cognition. A further connection has also been pointed out when the question of the phenomena of the small child being entirely an organ of perception arose. There we could establish the remarkable line of development whereby the pure perception of the small child changes approximately at the seventh year into imaginative thinking, and then further into conceptual thinking. Thought processes develop out of processes of perception. Perception proves here again as the primary function, as the first step of thinking. In this connection it is also important to keep in our consciousness a further, already-mentioned fact, namely, that the front part of the brain, the physical basis of the intellect, is essentially a transformed organ of smell.

This has arisen through transformation and enlargement of the nerves associated with smelling. Here again there is revealed a strange connection between sense organism and thought-organism, between the two apparently different functions of perception and thinking. That the process of perception influences the process of thinking is easily seen. But is the opposite also possible, namely that the development of the brain and nervous system, and in connection with this, our thinking, influenced our sense processes in the course of time? Anthroposophy answers this question in the affirmative. It shows how the progressive development of brain and nervous system benumbs the sense processes ever more strongly. Through this our perception becomes paler and deteriorates. This development of the nervous system and its centre, the brain, makes the experience of the sensory qualities weaker and less real. Steiner actually speaks of death processes which, from the nervous system, play into the sense processes.

> In fact, the task of the optic nerve is not to carry the colour-impressions back to the brain but to extinguish them at a certain point … Towards the brain, the optic nerves, auditory nerves and the nerves of warmth reduces everything they had on the periphery down to a faint shadow.[9]

Steiner goes on to say that in future the senses will be still further deadened by the brain, and regarding perceiving the outer world, humankind is heading towards an ever greater desolation and emptiness.

Regarding the eye, it can happen that subtle nuances of colour can no longer be perceived or distinguished, for instance in an evening sky. The development of our sensory organs has not nearly reached its goal. Humanity faces the choice to allow the deterioration to continue, or to consciously develop the sense organism to a higher level. 'If organs are not actually used for their purpose, they die off.'[10]

The other danger threatening the sense organism comes from technical achievements. The human spirit has created, in addition to the world of nature, two additional worlds – the world of technology and the world of art. Contemporary human beings live, or at least can live, in three worlds:

The world of art
The world of nature
The world of technology

Now somewhat unusual questions could conceivably be asked such as, what kind of sense impressions are given to us by these three very different worlds? Are they equal, or are there essential differences, perhaps of a qualitative nature? Which world gives us particularly enlivening, invigorating sense impressions? Which of these three worlds injures our sense organism?

Such questions are worth investigating. Let us leave out nature for the time being. We accept nature's sense impressions as a given fact and as beneficial. Let us keep initially to the world of technology and its achievements. Technology has created an absolutely artificial environment, far from nature, with particular effects upon the sense organism. We are not making any value judgments. Nevertheless it is good to be conscious of the fact that, in order to build the realm of technology, our connection with nature has first to be destroyed to a considerable degree, whether we are engaging with wood or stone, quarries or forests, earth, water or air. In this way raw materials are produced which are needed to set up the world of machines. Taking such facts for granted, let us try and consider the effects which proceed from technical surroundings upon man, first of all upon the growing human being, the child. Generally speaking it can be said, and every intimate observation confirms this, that compared with that which nature has to offer us, the technical world is a cold one.

This world does not give us a vigorous life and soul warmth. Because of this, quite obvious deficiencies occur in the human being. A kind of malnutrition of the soul can be observed. Furthermore, facing these deficiencies there now stands a tremendous flood of aggressive sense impressions which we can characterize as over-stimulation. Here we are obviously concerned with sense impressions qualitatively different from those which nature presents to us. Technology has in no way a direct effect upon the level of morality, but in a striking way it affects the sense organism of the human being. Technology is aggressive, bringing disorder and harm. The technical achievements used in everyday life, right into every detail of daily routine, will increase in future.

No sensible person will want to stop the wheel of progress in the field of technology. But a certain question which particularly concerns the educator arises here. What is to be done to meet the dangers which in this way threaten the sense organism? Before we try to answer this question we shall present three examples showing how the technical life of civilization can work on the three groups of senses.

Let us begin with the will senses. With our sense of movement we also perceive movements outside us. It would be unrealistic to imagine that movement is movement regardless of where it comes from and how it has started, that the effect upon human beings would remain the same. With such a groundless belief we could not comprehend reality. The fish in the water, the bird in the air, the deer in the meadow, the clouds in the sky: we can perceive them all in their movements. It is nature which produces these living processes of movement and conveys them to our senses. Leaving aside any prejudice, if we compare these with movements of a mechanical kind, which have been caused by a motor, one can experience quite an impressive difference. Technology has produced, among other things, movements of quite a special kind.

Let us think of the complicated technical processes that produce movement on the screen or on television. These are movements which no longer have the slightest connection with natural ones. However, these are movements which we are always forced to take part in, if only in the most delicate way. Every kind of mechanical movement appeals to our sense of movement (and with it our entire organism of movement) in quite a different way than the movements of nature. The same applies to all the other will senses.

Let us consider the effect of technology upon the cognitive senses, taking as one example the sense for the I. When listening to the radio or television, no I is present. We hear a voice, but the human being whom we should like to connect with this voice is not present. For the child the radio takes the place of the I-endowed human being. This is by no means meant ironically. But if we consider how children, let us say at the beginning of the twentieth century, experienced a human being, a coach driver, the milkman, the town crier, a beggar, and so on, with all their senses, above all with their germinal sense of I, then we acquire an idea of the loss children suffer if they are submitted too much to the mass media. Here the loss becomes clearly visible. The same could be shown for the other three cognitive senses.

And what is the situation with regard to the middle senses? Think of the exhaust fumes filling the towns, of the foodstuffs which have lost their original taste through all sorts of adulteration; think of the glaring illuminated advertisements, and again of television, then the answers to such questions are not difficult to find. We mention such dangers only with the intention of showing the educational possibilities of meeting them.

3.3 Enlivening and ensouling the sense organism

Is there a way to protect the sense organism from the dangers which threaten it? Are there possibilities not only of preventing the decline in which it is at present, but also of reinvigorating it to develop towards its true goal? Recalling the inexorable law, that organs which are not used for their purpose 'die off'; what now would be the first step on the way to achieving those goals? In what follows we are concerned – and this must be emphasized – with the adult human being. The pedagogical aspect will be discussed in the last chapter. In general, for the time being we can say as an answer to such questions, that the sense processes must experience a renewal of life and also, most of all, an ensoulment.

Man will raise the dead sense process which he has today, and transform it into something living. Rudolf Steiner comments, 'In a certain way the sense processes again become regions of life.'[11]

> Therefore we must completely metamorphose our sense organs. In their finer structure they must become something quite different to what they have been ... We have, for instance, to learn to feel how the will works through our eye.

What possibilities are offered by anthroposophy to the adult in order to come nearer to this aim of enlivening and ensouling the sense processes? There are three possibilities. For the time being let us mention them as hints:

A strengthened, spiritualized thinking,
The becoming aware of phenomena as
    Goethe suggested,
Artistic activity and enjoyment

Let us consider the first possibility, the active or spiritualized thinking. As has already often been pointed out, a certainly hidden, but nevertheless very close, connection between sense processes and thought processes does exist. If a dried up, merely intellectual thinking can bring forth dying processes in the sense organism, then through active thinking, enlivening forces can flow into the sense processes. This is because in this strengthened or pure thinking there lives the rejuvenating element of the will. As the pure intellect is, more or less, withered will, so that kind of thinking of which Steiner speaks, a thinking which is freshly enlivened and rejuvenated by will forces, is beneficial to the sense organism.

We know that the ancient Greeks still possessed a very intense sensory life, which enabled them to be vitally connected with nature. The cause for this was that in their enlivened and spiritualized bodily nature they had a surplus of forces which worked into their sense organism. The body of present day people no longer possess such a surplus of life, and are hardened and dried up. Present day people have to seek for another way to develop their sense organism. They have to enliven it again out of the soul and spirit. For this it is necessary to gain the faculty to penetrate into the soul and spirit realm through thinking. The path of modern human beings consequently has to be a different one from that of ancient Greeks, just to mention an example. The abundant vitality of life forces emanating from the physical body of the ancient Greeks affected their eyes and ears and other sense organs. Today we have to awaken such vitality in our soul and spirit that it can work into our senses.

Let us turn to the second possibility of changing the sense organism, namely, schooling ourselves in becoming aware of pure phenomena, as shown by Goethe's example. As before we spoke of pure thinking, so now we turn to the opposite pole, that of pure perception. Goethe was indeed a genius as an observer, consciously training the vitality of his powers of observation so that they were akin to those of a young child or of the ancient Greeks. Goethe claimed that 'every new object, well contemplated, opens up a new organ of perception within us.' With such powers of 'contemplating well' the human being takes hold of the sense organ with enhanced will-activity and thus really enters into the surrounding world. If we develop insufficient love for the phenomena, prematurely using the combining ability of reasoning, then we involve ourselves too quickly in judgment and theories, and through this become estranged to the world of phenomena.

Goethe wished to cognize the pure phenomena, the primal phenomena, through willed perception, in order to unite himself with them. He was of the opinion that through such an attitude the phenomena would reveal their essential nature, would pronounce their secrets.

Reason itself should only serve to distinguish more complicated phenomena from the primal phenomena, and to relate one phenomenon with another. What Goethe did not actually pursue were the abstract laws of nature, because through them only finished, lifeless nature could be captured. He strove for the living, the growing in nature. Goethe never regarded 'contemplating well' otherwise than as an active perception, a perceiving in which the will pours into the sense processes as a rejuvenating element. Steiner tells us that,

> what Goethe wishes humankind to search for is pure perception. And he only wanted reason to be used in order to assemble the phenomena in such a way that they can pronounce their secrets themselves. Goethe wanted to have a natural science free from hypothesis, free from the combining reason. This is also the foundation of his theory of colours. The point in question was not at all understood. Because Goethe wished that deductive reasoning should hold back from theoretical speculation about the perceptions, in order to take another route.[12]

A third way to further develop the sense organism is rooted in every artistic activity. The healthy enjoyment and observation of art is also beneficial to the human being. An impressive fact stands before us. The creative human being has added to the world of nature the worlds of technology and art. The advantages which technology provides for us are legion, beyond estimation. But the same grand technology works like a constant attack upon our twelve senses. Surrendered solely to this technical world, the sense organism would fall ill and disintegrate. If nature has a beneficial effect on the sense organism, then the world of art has an amazingly greater positive effect. It is as if this world was created to make good again and again in the sense organism what has been damaged by the world of technology. We can only live without harm in a technological world if we recognize the healing effect of artistic occupation and enjoyment, and live accordingly.

To close this section, here is another quote from Steiner:

> The real aesthetic attitude of man consists in the fact that the sense organs in a certain way become enlivened and the life processes ensouled. This is a very important truth about man, because it gives us an understanding for many things. We have to look for that stronger life in the sense organs and different life of the realm of the senses, than is usually the case in art and in the enjoyment of art. And it is just the same with the life processes which become more ensouled through artistic enjoyment than in ordinary life. Because in our materialistic age these things are not considered according to reality, the significance of the complete change which happens to man when he stands in the artistic realm cannot fully be laid hold of.[13]

4. Cultivating the Sense Organism Through Education

4.1 Stages of lessons that cultivate perception

With regard to the twelve senses, in every lesson we turn primarily to the sense organism of the child. There is no educational measure which does not appeal to the one or other group of senses belonging to the children. Steiner's statement that we have to approach the child through the senses, refers to this. Looked at in this way, all teaching would actually be a lesson that call on children's senses, The purpose of these lessons is to lay a foundation in the soul of the children to create an inner connection between them and the surrounding world. What is in question here is the inner perception as preliminary step to the outer perception. We shall discuss the stages of these lessons throughout all the primary school years by way of some examples. But before this, a word from Steiner about what were customary 'object lessons' (or *Anschauungsunterricht* in German) at the beginning of the twentieth century.

> It is also important to cultivate object lessons in our school, but without allowing them to become banal. The children should never have

the feeling that what they are being told in an object lesson is really rather obvious. 'Here is a piece of chalk. What colour is it?' – 'Yellow.' 'What is it like at the top?' – 'It is broken off.' Many an object lesson is given along these lines. It is atrocious. Something that is obvious in ordinary life should not be used as an object lesson. Such lessons should be lifted up to a higher level. When they are being given an object lesson, the children should be transported by it to a higher sphere of their soul life.[1]

What could a first such lesson cultivating the senses in a Class One look like? What should be taken into consideration, what educational intention could be combined with such teaching? The aim of this lesson must indeed be the drawing of the children's attention to their immediate environment as well as to the wider one and to awaken the children to the world into which they have been born. The teacher's task is to awaken the children to all that lives and works around them in plants, animals and human beings, in mountains and rivers. This is the child's earthly home, with which he is to become familiar in the right way. Steiner consequently called this main lesson 'home surroundings'. Although as a school subject this study only appears a few years later, this very first study in home surroundings, meaning the cultivation of perception, has an entirely different character for seven- and eight-year-old children than for older children. Here it is essential to observe a principle that can be expressed as 'inner perception has to precede the outer'. We can also imagine a lesson which unites the inner perception with the outer. What is to be brought to the child at this age regarding facts and occurrences in nature has to be formed in the following way.

Something living and ensouled must stimulate the living and ensouled being of the child to active, inner perception that can then harmonize with the outer perception. In a certain sense we are dealing with an artistically formed study of home surroundings. It has pictorial, symbolic character and just because of this it is particularly close to the inner truths of the facts of nature. For example, the relationship of the bee to the flower is such an intrinsic part of nature, as is the relationship of the butterfly or the bumblebee to the flower.

These three related but nevertheless, very different, natural phenomena can be given to the children in pictorial story form, so that later, perceiving such a process out in nature, they can experience it with much greater interest and understanding than would otherwise be the case. Through such study of home surroundings, of what is familiar, children's observation becomes more refined and intimate.

If you are to educate a child of this age, you have to develop the artistic sense to enliven everything. The teacher has to let the plants speak, let the animals behave morally ... The ideal is that out of the teacher himself, as his individual creation, there arises a conversation between plants, that the fairytale between lily and rose is created by the teacher himself through his imaginative insight. Likewise the conversation of the sun with the moon ... What you create yourself still possesses forces of growth, fresh life which affects the child. Everything the child learns about plants, animals, minerals, about the sun and moon, mountains and rivers, should actually stream in this form to the end of the ninth year, because the child unites himself with the world. World and child, child and world is one thing at this age.[2]

Between the ninth and the tenth year, as already mentioned, a decisive change in the child's development takes place. Here we can observe the very first stirrings of appropriate intellectual thinking. Connected with this development is the other fact that the life forces of the sense organism slightly withdraw. As a result of such changes the children consider the world differently than hitherto. The effect of this development is the opening up of an abyss between the individual child and the surrounding world. The child no longer experiences being connected to the world in such an intensive manner as before. Children not only face the surrounding world but also experience it as being more differentiated. The various spheres of nature contrast more strongly. The task of education is to prevent this development process from setting in too early or in or in an inappropriate way. In this case further physical-soul-spiritual development of the child cannot take place healthily. The teaching must also do justice to the new consciousness of the child. This surrounding world has to be described to the child in quite a new way, no longer in the imaginative way just referred to, though nevertheless in a lively manner imbued with feeling.

We could say that a step has to be made from the prevailing inner perception to the outer. Until now there was a more imaginative comprehension of the surrounding world, and after this change there is a more feeling-like experience. What is now to be the centre of this new 'object lesson'? Now, at about nine or ten years of age, the children should, for the first time, look more closely at the activities of the human being, the tools, and fruits of labour. The children are to see the work of the farmer, the plough and the other tools he uses. They learn to distinguish, just to give an example, the various kinds of cereals. They also experience how mortar is prepared, how a wall, a house in built. The children must look so closely that they can recount what they have seen. In this way they are led from the foundation of the moral-soul element to practical reality. To perceive all this, the children need their entire, differentiated sense organism. The difference in the ability to observe between the first two school years and the third is impressive.

The way which leads from inner perception via outer perception to abstract conception can be shown especially well by taking the example of sun, moon and stars. What kind of world picture should this be, to correspond with the cognitive qualities of children before the tenth year? As we know, children of this age still possess the faculty of inner, pictorial perceptions. With the help of this faculty they can also understand all the cosmic processes as long as they are brought in a pictorial-mythical form. They 'see' these pictures and understand them. All true myths appeal to a consciousness in which picture and thought are still one. The very first teaching of astronomy cannot be anything else but mythology. The myths which the teacher is to use need not always be ancient, but can be created by himself. He can be inspired by poets of more recent days who have put such myths into short poems, for example, Christian Morgenstern's Song of the Sun:

> I am the Sun and I bear with my might
> The Earth by day, the Earth by night.
> I hold her fast and my gifts I bestow
> That everything on her may live and grow.

Such a lesson in astronomy awakens in children confidence and trust. Children with their imaginative perception can understand it.

After the tenth year, astronomy may take on a different feature. The time has come when we can appeal in the lessons to the children's sense perception, that is, to their own observation. The following questions should only point to the character of this second stage of astronomy. Looking from your house, where has the sun risen today? Behind which hill did it set yesterday? What path has the sun described from dawn to dusk? Does it describe the same path the whole year round? At night the stars appear. If you look at them for some length of time, you will notice how they move across the night sky. A great deal is achieved if the children experience through observation how the stars rise slanting in the east and describing an arc, and move to the west. In contrast, the stars in the north (or in the south in the southern hemisphere) descend from above, move from the west to the east, some constellations disappearing beneath the horizon in order to reappear later, others describing a circle, whose centres lie high above the earth. In this way the attention of the children is directed to the phenomena, even if only through descriptions by the teacher.

In a certain sense the children experience in their development what once the whole of humankind has passed through. The original world picture of man was mythological. It was succeeded by the Ptolemaic world picture (with the earth in the centre), which is characterized by the transition from inner perception (intuitive knowledge) to outer sense perception. It is important to know that the mythical and Ptolemaic world pictures were not opposed to each other, but that they lived peacefully side-by-side, and for the Greeks possessed equal validity.

The one world picture did not extinguish the other, did not make it into an error. The Ptolemaic world picture indeed starts from a point of view that is still spiritual and allows space for the supersensible element. Outer sense perceptions and spiritual perception are still in harmony. Because he used his senses, this kind of perception produced in the human being a healthy self-confidence. The same still happens today with children, if we allow them to perceive a world picture based on pure sense perception.

It can happen that three groups of children appear in a class which is led to the phenomena in the skies in the way just described. For one group this way of observation is new. These are the somewhat dreamy children who still have a distinct longing for the pictorial element, who would like to dwell upon this inner perception. They would like to continue hearing myths, fairytales and stories for astronomy. Nevertheless they are willing to use their senses in order to be able to learn with their help. Children in the second group from the very beginning are already more awake in their senses. The new way of observation meets their openness to the sense world. Then there may also be a third group of children; the smaller it is, the better. They are those children in whom all perceptions are already haunted by the Copernican sun-centred picture, often in a most distorted way. These perceptions make it difficult for the children to approach the phenomena using their senses. Such children prove themselves to be disinclined to observe the course of sun and moon, or the movements of the stars in the heavens.

In the lessons the children should not be acquainted with the Copernican world picture before their twelfth year. Frequently it is too little considered just what a mighty jump it was for humankind to proceed from the Ptolemaic to the Copernican way of observation. Humankind underwent a process of abstraction which was also a step toward freedom, freedom which was bought at the expense of losing the divine. Nicolaus Copernicus, the representative of the new world picture, hesitated for thirty-six years before making his life's work public. Then the effect was indeed tremendous. Martin Luther, for example, wrote about Copernicus: 'This fool wishes to turn the whole art of astronomy upside down. But as the Holy Bible indicates, Joshua commanded the sun to remain still, and not the earth.' Philipp Melanchthon, Luther's collaborator wrote, 'Wise rulers should have curbed such light-mindedness.' But what does Goethe say about the Copernican world-system?

Perhaps there has never been made a greater demand on humankind. How much went up into fog and smoke: a second paradise, a world of innocence, poetry, piety, the witness of the senses, the conviction of a poetic-religious creed. No wonder that people were unwilling to let all this go, that there was opposition to such a doctrine in every possible way, a doctrine which challenged those who accepted it to freedom of outlook and greatness of opinion hitherto unknown.[3]

A question of the educator: should such a hitherto unknown freedom of view and greatness of conviction be expected from eight- and nine-year-old children?

Has the Copernican world system the character of eternity, one could ask. We do not think so. Einstein once wrote that the progress of science, whereby he referred mostly to his theory of relativity, has not left untouched the idea of Copernicus, which seems so clear to everyone. Yet the discovery of Copernicus could perhaps one day become meaningless, as indeed may the whole conflict between the followers of Ptolemy and Copernicus. But if we investigate what the world picture of Einstein is, as opposed to that of Copernicus, one learns that the most striking difference lies in the fact that Einstein was more mathematical, and nothing of the realm of perception was present at all. It is reported that Einstein appeared in a meeting of scholars and said, 'Here in my briefcase I have the world picture of the future.' By this he meant his general and final 'world formula', he had brought with him and which excels itself by an absolute absence of any picture.

At the age of twelve children are mature enough for the first physics lesson. Through it they experience a quite new in principle, and that is the *experiment*. Experimentation, as a method of research, began in the sixteenth century and was primarily developed by Francis Bacon. Bacon asserted that 'we must put nature to the rack and force her to bear testimony.' Indeed, by using this methodology, we create artificial situations, thereby forcing nature to disclose herself. In contrast to the use of experiments stands the observation of nature.

The observer of nature receives what it pleases nature to disclose to him. He must practise patience; he must be able to wait. The one who experiments cannot do otherwise, as it lies in the nature of the experiment, than to look impatiently to the results. The observer of nature must develop a more intimate connection to nature than the one who experiments. The experiment leads to quick results, which is also why the jump from the phenomena to the laws of nature is so short and quick and perhaps also occasionally a premature one – an objection that Goethe raised. An essential feature of the experiment is that it also becomes separated from the human being, that it misleads man to rely completely on the apparatus and to trust himself too little, that is, his sense organism. Goethe again drew attention to this circumstance:

> Man in himself, in as far as he uses his healthy
> senses, is the greatest and most precise physical
> apparatus which can exist, and this is just the
> greatest misfortune of the newer physics, that
> people as it were separated the experiments
> from man and only wished to recognize nature
> in that which artificial instruments show.[4]

Goethe, the inspired observer and researcher of nature, can to a great extent be a teacher, concerning the best method of teaching.

There is no doubt that as soon as children have become sufficiently mature, they must be led to natural science experiments. In a certain sense even Goethe experimented, as his studies of optics prove. It would be a great mistake if the teacher did not demonstrate in the children's first optics lessons, the exemplary methods of observation which Goethe pioneered in his theory of colour. Goethe used as apparatus a three-sided glass prism and little black-and-white cards. Inspired by this Goethean way of experimenting, we can allow the children to look through prisms and describe their new experience. This is an excellent exercise in observing and describing, and a great experience for the children.

One can thus put into words for the children how the exciting and at first chaotic array of colours begins to take shape and be ordered and to express laws. If we hold the prism in a certain way before our eyes, we see coloured bands in those places where darkness and light join. If the light is above the dark, we see the blue-violet colours extending into the dark area. If however the dark is above the light, then we see red-yellow colours in the light area. But if the two different colour-bands meet, if they cover one another to a small extent, then we get a wide band with all the rainbow colours.

We can observe two different kinds of such wide bands. On the one hand green is added through mixing the yellow of the one colour-band with the blue of the other. Magenta or peach blossom arises as a new colour where the violet of the one and the red of the other colour-band meet. The colours therefore arise where light and darkness meet. The prism is the thing which through its strange form makes the light and the dark areas overlap a little. The colours therefore arise through a play of light and darkness. Colours, as Goethe said, are the 'deeds and sufferings of the light.' The wide colour-band with the seven rainbow colours, the 'colour spectrum', is for Goethe a derived, secondary phenomenon. Primary phenomena however are for him the two small colour-bands.

In this way children perceive an underlying law, and they know beforehand when the one or the other colour-band will appear, or under which circumstances the one or the other complete colour spectrum will appear.

Steiner has given definite pointers regarding methods of experimentation in the physics and chemistry lessons for the middle and upper classes. From the point of view of the sense organism these pointers are most revealing. This method of observing leads the pupils to healthy perception. For such an intensive, strenuous observation the whole human being and the whole sense organism is required.

A decisive question of method is as follows: is it best immediately after the experiment to lead the pupils to the postulated law of nature? This would mean that the attention of the young person would be swiftly drawn away from observing the phenomena in order to set *thinking* in its place. A properly understood teaching of the senses explains why Steiner did not recommend such a method. His suggestions rather recommend removing the apparatus and instruments after the experiment, allowing the pupils to recall in a free manner all the observed processes, and then waiting to extract the laws of nature until the following day. This avoids the activity of thinking overwhelming the phenomena in an over-hasty manner. Between the observation and the deduction of laws of nature there is the time of sleep. This is not without significance. Only on the following day is the pupil inwardly ready to think about the perception. Now the pupils feel the need to use their reason, in order consciously to digest what was perceived the previous day.

One of the many educational tasks that falls to a teacher is, over the years to enable the pupils to become capable of expressing their observations either orally or in writing. In order to observe correctly any occurrence in our surroundings to which we are witnesses, the foremost condition is the regular exercising of the sense organism. This is not sufficient by itself. To this is added the mastery of language which must serve us to be able to pass on what has been observed. And a third condition joins the other two. It is not at all easy even with a proper faculty of observation and a tolerable command of language to reproduce an objective occurrence so that nothing inadmissibly subjective creeps in as something of our personal opinions and judgments, wishes, intentions, sympathies and antipathies. It is easy to give ourselves up to illusions if we take it for granted that we can objectively describe a fact. Statements by eyewitnesses in court, for example, reveal clearly what has not been developed in education: the training to observe well and to express well, but most of all the love of truth. The report of the experiment consequently has the task to develop these three faculties in a proper way. With regard to this theme we quote from Steiner:

> It should be seen to that our society is so
> developed that we can rely more on witnesses
> and that people speak more truthfully. In order
> to achieve this a start has to be made already
> in childhood. That is why it is so important
> that what has been seen and experienced is

retold, more so than the fostering of free essay writing. In this way the habit is implanted in the children to tell the truth in life as well as in the courtroom ... The free essay does not yet really belong to the primary school. But the retelling of reading material, of what has been heard, does belong to the primary school, because children have to take this in, for otherwise they cannot partake socially in the right way in society.[5]

4.2 Cultivating living thinking

We have already touched on the connections between the quality of thinking and the quality of perception. We have also pointed out how an activated thinking, strengthened by the will, can produce a regenerating effect upon the sense organism. Can we apply such an indication given by Steiner for adults to the educational realm? Can we speak at all of a living thinking with younger schoolchildren?

By contrasting such thinking to the intellectual thinking of the adult, we are led to the fact that schoolchildren actually exercise a very vivid childlike thinking. This faculty must not be developed in a precocious and unhealthy way, so that it can remain as childlike fantasy, imaginative thinking. and so on. It is still a spiritualized thinking, in as much as it is an organ of perception for spiritual truths in pictures. In lessons we have to work with this fantasy life of the child. The spiritual truths which children are able to perceive in a thinking manner are all the genuine myths, parables, fairytales, legends and fables. All original myths are not products of artistic fantasy. As expressions of real imaginations, their sources lie deeper. For this reason young schoolchild must live for a time in this kind of thought-world in order to be able to develop their thinking further.

4.3 Cultivating the will senses

For the child, the development of the will senses has three aspects. The first is that the will forces and the will senses of the child are interdependent and the one cannot be developed without the other.

Secondly it is necessary to be aware of the fact that the proper development of the cognitive senses, by which children learn in school, is bound up with a well-developed will sense. It is good to repeatedly recall the fact that the cognitive senses originated through metamorphosis of the will senses. A healthy development of the cognitive senses in the child presupposes a healthy lower sense organism.

The fostering of the will senses has a third educational aspect. It has already been mentioned that the perception of the four will senses is generally subconscious. For example, we are not capable of establishing what the sense of life in our organs, in the liver, the spleen, the heart and so on, really perceives, or what takes place in the muscles when we move. All perceptions of the will senses remain in the subconscious, but something of what is perceived in a concealed way radiates into our life of feeling, a fact that has already been mentioned in the discussion on the sense of life. When I remark about myself that I feel refreshed, rested or comfortable; or that I feel uncomfortable, that something does not seem right with my stomach or my heart – then this usually concerns perceptions of the lower senses which have risen into the life of feeling. The experiences of these senses consequently influence my life of feeling, even when I am not able to raise anything of these life processes into my consciousness. Concerning the sense of life, we feel comfort or discomfort. From the educational point of view it is desirable that the children live in a feeling of well-being, brought about through healthy, organic processes.

What kinds of feelings are evoked by the perceptions of the three different will senses? Anthroposophy gives important information for education. This can be confirmed through self-observation, through observing children and through realistic thinking. Let us begin with the effect of the *sense of our own movement*. Steiner describes it in the following way:

> Whether we jump or dance, we perceive
> whether and how we move. Radiated into
> the soul, this gives that feeling of freedom in
> human being which enables them to experience
> themselves as a soul ... That you experience
> yourself as a free soul is due to the radiation of
> the sense of movement, that is, the raying in of
> the muscular contractions and extensions into
> your soul.[6]

As educators, however, let us be aware that this feeling of freedom can never occur if human beings, in our case, children, do not express themselves in movements according to human nature. If the movements are robot-like, possess mechanical character, or have been copied from machines, then in the soul-life there arises the counterpart of the feeling of freedom: the feeling of compulsion in regard to human thinking and acting.

The *sense of balance* which takes part in every physical activity awakens a further kind of feeling in the human being:

> How do we feel the experience of the sense of balance radiated into the soul? We experience it as that inner tranquillity which causes us, when walking from here to there, not to leave behind the person who is in my body, but I take him along; he remains the same. After all, I don't leave myself behind today, but am the same tomorrow. This independence from the body is the result of the raying in of the sense of balance into the soul. It engenders the feeling of being a spirit.[7]

If we are able to keep ourselves physically in balance, this creates the feeling of inner security and certainty. It creates the capacity not to lose our inner balance, our equanimity, so easily in later life. The counter-picture would be the feeling of dependence on the body and on all sorts of matters in life and an inner uncertainty caused by it.

Education of the feeling-like effects of the experiences of the *sense of touch* leads to surprising results. If I touch anything of nature I touch something which is not the result of human work, something that has rather been created by divine forces. I touch the wool of a sheep, I caress the fur of a cat, my hand moves over silk or velvet, I touch the bark of a tree, a rose petal. Every time I touch something which has its origin in divine-creative activity, my soul-life, without my necessarily becoming aware of it, is filled, stimulated with feelings of a special kind.

> What in this way radiates into the centre and
> what is experienced outwardly is nothing other
> than being penetrated by the feeling of God.
> Man without the sense of touch would not
> have the feeling of God ... [The sense of touch
> feels roughness, smoothness, softness, hardness as
> radiating to the periphery,] what is reflected into
> the soul, that is the penetration by the general
> universal–substance.

The experience through the sense of touch is 'divine substance penetrating everything.'[8]

But if such experiences of touch have never or only scarcely been experienced in childhood, this feeling of God spoken of here will only be able to develop in a limited fashion. This could be the case, for example, if children were only surrounded by artificial fibres. Artificial fibres are indispensable for modern life; they are dispensable in the life of children. The feelings described here, including the feeling of comfort, are most precious, even religious feelings. We rightly develop such feelings in children when in lessons we have them use their bodies in a healthy, that is, in a human way.

Special attention to the development of the will senses has to be given at an early school age. The present age demands such cultivation. Parents and teachers have increasingly to reckon with the fact that present civilization is not kindly disposed to the development of children.

The number of children who before their seventh year have been harmed in some way by modern civilization is particularly great. The phenomenon of maladjusted children is frequently spoken about. We are of the opinion that the surroundings in which the children grow up has caused harm and that the school has to put right this damage. From the point of view of education, we live in a degenerated society, having, over the course of decades, created unsuitable surroundings for children.

The character of our age is determined by technology and our entire outer life down to every detail is becoming in ever increasing measure technical. The prototype of technology is the machine. The running machine represents movement which takes place by compulsion, according to strict mechanical laws. This is not the kind of movement which is able to create feelings of freedom when we are confronted by it with our sense organism. Children today live in the midst of this world. Children are fascinated by motorized movements, but through these movements their will senses as well as their whole will nature, are being attacked. Seen from this point of view three important educational tasks arise.

Three educational tasks

I should like to call the first 'cherish and protect'. This is initially to benefit the small child. By 'cherish' we mean the preserving and protecting of small children from the attack of technological forces. Young children are by no means equal to such an attack, not physically, nor from the point of view of their soul, nor according to their stage of consciousness. Such cherishing and protecting is not completely possible, but it is possible to a great extent. We can avoid subjecting young children to such things as, for instance, television, films and radio, for we know how much damage has already been caused to children through them.

The second educational task has a healing character. The demand for a therapeutic element in education grows increasingly strong. Through educational measures the damage can be corrected and made good. Children affected by their environment can be healed by the healthy influence of education.

The third task, however, is completely directed towards the future. It starts with the insight that today children have to be furnished with quite different strengths and abilities than hitherto, so that as adults they not only cope with the increasing complexities of civilization, but that they can master the challenges they will face.

The importance of rhythm

Now that we have listed three great educational tasks, we return to an important question. Which kind of activity is best for counteracting today's technologically dominated life? Old children's games such as ring games, with their often apparently senseless, nevertheless rhythmic little verses and rhymes, are a wonderful training of the lower senses! Or for example, skipping with a rope, where two children swing the rope and a third has to jump. Let us observe this child, how their whole body takes part in the rhythm of the rope, even before they jump in, how they then have to jump off the ground, fly up, experience for a short moment the absence of gravity, return back to the ground, now having to keep their balance, and jumping off the ground again the next moment.

In such a child's jumping all four will senses enter into a celebration. And their feeling life blossoms in the most beautiful way. A feeling of comfort, pleasure, freedom and inner security are all experienced by the child in this activity.

In truth, all these children's games were once the actual 'high school' for children's will senses. Their value was and still is incomparable. They certainly were once given to children by people who knew something about the underlying secrets of these games. Then seven-year-old children came to school with well-developed will senses. Even if the teaching was then intellectual, perhaps not particularly good, it did not matter so much. The situation today is quite different. The cultivation of the will senses has to be taken over by the school. This is an urgent task. How we can best appeal to the will senses and cultivate them through our teaching. In answering this question we enter the realm of educational practice. Of course, only a very small part of what could be said about it can be given here.

Every time we allow the children to use their bodies in a healthy way, we appeal to the will senses, cultivating them. Generally speaking, it is important to emphasize movement that is alive and human, rather than today's prevalent lifeless motor-like movement that is quite unchildlike. Every sense-enriching action also engages, via the will senses the will nature, be it the young child's playful activity, the artistic activity of the schoolchild or the handicraft of the young person. An especially important kind of movement is that which is rhythmical. Everything of a rhythmical nature contains a special energy. Therefore everything rhythmical, for which the child shows proclivity during the school age, serves the cultivation of the lower senses. Rhythm can ensoul and form that which tends toward numbness, toward automation; movement characteristic of rhythm can both calm and enliven.

Often, however, what is called rhythm is envisaged too narrowly. It is justified to speak of rhythm in a far wider sense than is usually the case. There is a rhythm of the day, the week, the year, a life rhythm, and so on. The whole human being is inclined towards rhythm. Rhythm is of special importance for all education. All these different rhythms are perceived by the will senses.

In past ages this rhythmical element lived most strongly in the educational elements of folk culture. In this way the people became educated through this appeal to their will nature. This was one of the effects of the repeated festivals of the year. Precisely through these rhythmical repetitions in religious activities, the will nature of the human being is appealed to. Think of the daily prayer, the morning verse, the daily or weekly reading of the same text, and so on. The constant repetitions in old texts (as for example the life and teachings of Buddha, or the refrains in fairytales) appearing to the mere intellect as senseless, regain their original significance through this consideration. They all exercise quite a special effect through rhythmical repetition.

However, our intellectual age is focused on occurrences that take place once only, on rapidly passing images and ideas, whereby each new picture immediately extinguishes the previous one. We constantly look for amusement or relaxation but this is really a dispersion of consciousness which is the opposite of true composure. It is consequently vitally important to ensure that a general rhythmical element in the building up of lessons is pursued. Precisely because outer life today is so a-rhythmical, it is important in school to structure each morning, each day, each week and each year (with its celebrations and festivals) in a distinctly rhythmical way. The educational purpose therefore does not only lie in the content of what is brought to the children, but just as much in observing the vital rhythm within the whole school year.

The effect of different subjects

If we now look at the individual subjects with regard to their effects on the will senses, we think first of gymnastics, because here quite obviously we are dealing with the body. All exercises, be they of a free nature or on apparatus, are so arranged that they call upon the activity of the will senses. The children are, in ever-changing ways, made to place themselves into space and to find their balance. Observe them, for example, running across a horizontal bar or perhaps across a fallen tree trunk, in the style of a tightrope walker. (Even better if you perform it yourself as a simple experiment.) You observe how they begin to move, place one leg in front of the other, and run. You can see how they carefully touch the narrow ledge with their feet, stretch their arms in order to keep balance, which threatens to be lost at any moment. At the end they reach secure ground with a jump, radiating a childlike self-reliance and inner well being, breathing deeply and feeling pleased.

However, in its extreme form sport forces such a one-sided fixed activity of the physical organism that the educational effect of children's games and healthy gymnastics cannot take place. What the lower senses have to experience when engaged in an extreme sporting activity has slipped away from the human realm, has taken on forceful character. It no longer works educationally in the will nature and is therefore not conducive to healthy feelings either. An effective activity for the lower senses can be found in what we could call running and drawing forms (as in form drawing). The point is to let the children of the lower classes perceive and experience all the geometrical, fundamental forms by stepping and running them themselves. They begin with the two fundamental elements of the straight and curved line. Out of these two elements all the possible geometrical forms and figures are derived. To run a straight line forwards and backwards is a healthy experience for children. To draw a vertical line on the blackboard calls upon their will organism.

In drawing such a line the children fetch it, so to speak, out of their bodies. It is written in the body, otherwise they could not walk upright. Something similar holds good for the horizontal. The children exercise all four will senses if they really run the geometrical forms of a circle, spiral, lemniscate and triangle. A further step then leads to the drawing of these forms. It is arm and hand which move, but their movements impart themselves in the most delicate way to the whole body. When drawing in this way the conceptual element is purposely kept back; with such activity children should be allowed to experience themselves unimpeded as a being of will. If we therefore name this kind of drawing a 'dynamic' one, in contrast to drawing something of a conceptual nature, like houses, trees, animals, and so on, then with this expression the nature of such an activity is easily defined. It would be an error to think that we are dealing here with abstract drawing, because we eliminate the sense perceptible element. These pure, fundamental forms are not abstractions and neither are the will nature and the body of the child.

Let us say a word here in passing about what is called

abstract art. Such a term actually does not affect the nature of this art. We rather meet here a pronounced dynamic element, the same element which we have before us in an original, simplest form in dynamic drawing. Kandinsky, the father of abstract painting said:

> A vertical line which combines with a
> horizontal creates almost a dramatic sound.
> The contract of the acute angle of a triangle
> with a circle has in fact no less an effect than
> God's finger touching the finger of Adam in
> Michelangelo [*Creation of Adam*].

Perpendicular, horizontal, angular and curved lines, and diagonals 'are forms of expressions of invisible power-impulses.'[9]

It is also important that children are not only allowed to run and draw such forms. To look at already created forms likewise has a definite effect. Each geometrical form has arisen out of movement and then has come to rest. But in looking at it, I lead it from myself back into movement. I can actually perceive a circle only by letting it arise for me. Therefore even in observing such geometrical forms through my 'sense of form' a dynamic element forms its basis With sense of form we do not encounter a new sense organ, but rather the combination of the four lower senses, especially the sense of movement and the sense of balance. The form drawing exercises where children symmetrically complete and mirror the missing half of the form appeals primarily to the sense of balance. Steiner suggested that children in Class 1 should run and draw many letter forms before the conventional meaning of these forms is taught. The letters are first allowed to appear as dynamic signs, as pure form elements which speak to the will senses. As soon as the child learns this sign means an 'A' and that a 'B', the will element gives way to the conceptual, which has little to do with the will nature of the child.

In a beautiful way all four will senses are enlivened through modelling and, somewhat less so, through woodcarving. Whoever has tried both these arts will soon have noticed that contemplation or thought about creating the best and most beautiful sculptural forms is of no special help. In contrast to painting, the significance of the sense of sight also recedes. It even can be a good exercise to once practise modelling blindly, deliberately to forego the sense of sight. The sense of touch becomes all the more active. The hand must continuously trace the planes and curves. We perceive all these planes, outlines and angles by moving our hands. The sense of balance is not inactive either. The sculptural forms must be weighed up, balance must be created in an artistic way, even if the form is not an especially symmetrical one. A sculptural work of art must have inner balance; only then does it give us security and satisfaction. All modelling is creating according to the organic laws, similar to the effectiveness of the archetypal plant, in Goethe's sense. For this reason the ensouled sense of life takes part in every artistically directed sculptural activity.

In this connection let us also point to the human, educational significance of artistic architecture. An ancient Greek, for example, who from time to time, or even every day, was able to see such a perfect work of art as a classical Greek temple was cultivated by it in his will sense organism. Simultaneously, religious feelings were implanted into his soul. Steiner refers to the therapeutic effect of artistic architecture from yet another aspect.

> Through merely looking out into nature, our soul perceives a certain configuration. It looks at nature and realizes that not all the needs of his seeing are satisfied. All this actually holds good for perception in its entirety. Certain remnants of perception remain dissatisfied if you merely look out into nature. If the human being constantly only looks at nature his soul deteriorates with regard to perception. He suffers soul-deterioration. This was known in earlier mystery wisdom, but it was also known in what way this deterioration is balanced. It was known that the temple architecture was the remedy against the deterioration of the senses, when these only looked out into nature. And when the Greek was led to his temple, where he saw the supporting and the weighing down elements; the columns, over them the architraves, and so on, when he perceived what confronted him as inner mechanics and dynamics, then his seeing became complete. The seeing became completed when he was faced with any architecture that was intended to catch this attention, to take it away from nature.[10]

It was the will organism of the Greek which was timed and cultivated by the temple architecture. Every artistically formed sculptural art has a similar significance as architecture. Such insights are particularly important for the lessons in the upper classes.

There are some subjects which in a measured way can serve simultaneously the cultivation of the upper as well as the lower senses. Foremost is music. Quite obviously we think first of the sense of sound or hearing which is fostered through singing and playing instruments. This sense of sound can, however, only perceive sounds but not sequences of sounds, not the rhythm underlying the music. Were we able to direct the sense of sound solely to music in arbitrary isolation as opposed to the other senses, the result would be a most one-sided, hardly imaginable sound experience. In order to perceive the sequence of notes, the rhythm, even the intervals, we unconsciously use the sense of our own movement and the sense of balance, two will senses. Consequently, through marching and parade music, for example, the will nature can be directly stirred to perform certain actions. On the other hand this music can serve to calm and ennoble the will nature. It was Orpheus who with his music tamed the wild animals. Our passionate animal nature can be restrained through music. We often speak of a musical sense. However, this musical sense is not a uniform sense organ, but the combination of the sense of sound and the two will senses mentioned above, movement and balance. This is similar to the sense for form, which is also not a uniform sense but a combination of the will senses with seeing.

We meet another combination of the upper and the lower senses in poetic recitation. Let us assume that we are listening to the recitation of a poem. Apart from its poetic language and pictorial quality, rhythm and rhyme are an essential characteristic of the poem. From this we can see how the sense of movement and sense of balance are engaged through poetry, especially in the recitation of poetry. The educational value of recitation lies in its ability to enliven and ensoul these two will senses.

> Each poem is so expressed that we perceive it through the sense of language. But if we turn only the sense of language to the poem, we will not understand it. Apart from the sense of language, the senses of balance and of movement must be directed in an ensouled way to the poem.

The content of a poem is not what is educationally most valuable. The content must not tyrannize the poetry. 'The perfect recitation is the one which emphasizes the musical element ... Poetry is not complete in the content, but in rhythm and rhyme.'[11]

The subject which appeals in the most effective way to the lower and the upper senses, which enlivens and ensouls them and thereby provides a first class medium for human education is eurythmy, the art of expressing sound through movement created by Rudolf Steiner.

When considering various subjects from the point of view of the strengthening of the will forces, geometry stands out. Geometry, as well as mathematics, arise from the correctly functioning lower senses, especially the senses of movement and balance. They form the primary foundation of knowledge, upon which everything else is built up. The fact that I can have ideas and concepts like perpendicular, horizontal, diagonal, straight, curved, circular and square, I owe to the objective perception of the lower senses.

The teaching of geometry begins in Class 1 and is to be carried through all the classes. Running and drawing geometrical forms and figures in the lower classes is nothing other than a practical, most visible teaching of geometry. It could almost be an educational requirement that the young schoolchild should first walk, as occurs in eurythmy, all these fundamental geometrical forms and afterwards draw them. What children at a later age construct in the geometry lessons with compass and ruler, they should previously, in a free manner, have moved and drawn. The contemplation and describing of these geometrical forms is, from the point of view of education, no less important than the drawing and constructing itself. The geometry lesson thus contributes significantly to the lessons that cultivate perception. Steiner says the following about the effect of a healthy, contemplative geometry lesson:

> The child is by all means to learn to look
> at angle, triangle, squares, and so on, in a
> descriptive way, and only at the age of twelve
> should you go on to proofs. Then the teacher
> will, through this element, counteract the
> chaotic tendencies which are always present in
> life.[12]

4.4 Cultivating the feeling senses

The middle senses give us the opportunity of perceiving what nature wishes to reveal to us regarding the sense perceptible world. We experience through these sense organs light and darkness, colours, smells, flavours, warmth and cold. Generally it can be said that natural surroundings appeal to our sense organism in a natural way too. Within certain limits we can say: what nature gives to us, we may enjoy. But the question still remains whether there is something like a natural cultivation of the middle senses through nature itself. A natural kind of sense care does exist.

To open children's eyes to the world of colours, to the coloured beauty of flowers and butterflies; to the wonder of the rainbow, and to the immensely delicate nuanced colour of an evening sky is of great importance. This wonderful world of colours in nature if well observed, exerts its enlivening effect upon the process of seeing. The teacher can stimulate the children in a lively way to observe the world of colours as nature conjures it up. However, the teacher himself must practise observation of nature, and have experience something of Goethe's sensory-moral effect of colours. The observation of the teacher is conveyed to the children.

Let us now turn to the other senses of this group. A healthy, unspoiled sense of taste is of great signifi-cance for the children. It is a task of the parents to do everything to prevent the children's sense of taste preserves a certain degree of refinement. Our sense of taste could, for instance, determine whether the food is really nourishing, or in spite of the beautiful appearance, almost worthless; whether this vegetable has grown on healthy or ruined ground; whether chemical ingredients have infringed upon the value of food; whether this or that is for me personally suitable or not, and so on. It is the sense of taste together with the sense of life which tells me whether I should stop eating or not. As a rule I then no longer enjoy the meal. In a certain limited way we are allowed to be gourmets. We subtly distinguish between the 'gour-mand' and the 'gourmet'. The former is a glutton who is most of all concerned with quantity. If a dish is according to his taste, he knows no limit. But he has actually spoiled his sense of taste. This is not the case with the gourmet, whose sense of taste has experienced a refinement.

In this connection a word about spices and herbs. They quite rightly play an important part in cooking and especially influence the human organism through the sense of taste. In rendering the meals aromatic, we flavour them and make them more wholesome. This is beneficial to our organism. When reluctantly and indifferently we consume a boring meal, the taste experience and with it the right participation of the physical organism in the digestion of the food are absent. Spices and herbs activate the formative forces working behind the experience of taste.

Each time a sense organ fails within a human being, a whole world is lost for him. This is most deeply experienced with the eye. But even when a more hidden organ, like the sense of smell, does not function correctly, the person concerned loses a great deal. How wonderfully refreshing it is for the whole organism to be able to experience and distinguish the different scents of roses, carnations, lilac, of lavender, rosemary and thyme, or the slightly less distinguishable scents of the various kinds of wood. How differently do animals smell, for example, dogs and cats, or the smells in a cow's stall and a horse's stable? To bring awareness of these nuances of plant and animal smells awakens the children's sense of smell in a good, natural way. There is no need to take it as far as, for example, Kodo, the Japanese art of incense appreciation, where in a special ceremony pleasantly scented woods are burned and the onlookers, or rather the 'on-smellers', enjoy the various wonderful fragrances. It is a kind of counterpart to the gourmet.

Regarding the sense of warmth, it is important that it functions on a natural basis in a healthy way. It expresses what is wholesome for us with regard to warmth in the same way as the sense of taste works with regard to food. The sense of warmth can however also be atrophied. This frequently happens through 'hardening attempts' of all kinds. If a boy runs about in the open with bare legs in ice cold weather, wearing short trousers, and actually does not feel the cold, this lack of sensitivity is a serious symptom of his sense of warmth having fallen into disorder.

When we spoke of the development of the middle senses in a natural way, we do so with the proviso that such refinement is limited, because the human being is not solely a nature being as is the animal. Limits are given to human beings through their spiritual nature. As human beings we cannot have either the sharpness of an eagle's eye or the refinement of a dog's nose.

In what way can the educator address the middle senses in his lessons? The teacher should work, not in the direction of nature, but towards the specifically human realm. Is there a world of experience, an artistic activity which takes hold of the work of nature and leads it further? We know that it belongs to the mission of art to enliven the sense organism. For instance, painting appeals in quite a special way to the middle sense organism, at least as far as the eye is concerned. The Swiss poet, Simon Gfeller, remarks in a lucid way in a note in his diary upon the effect of works of art upon the receptive onlooker.

Yesterday, after visiting the art exhibition in Berne, I made a strange observation: I was tired as a beaten dog, but going home I saw a hundred colourful motifs. Motifs everywhere, in spite of the dull, rainy weather. This is the effect: you receive new eyes. You learn to see ... You feel that you will never again be alone, but are united with tree and shrub, wood and meadow, sky and clouds. And you remember the art with great reverence and gratitude.[13]

Such a description shows us how our eyes, refreshed by viewing paintings, enable us to unite with nature in a far more lively way than had been previously possible. Looking with devotion at paintings heals the 'satiated perceptions in nature' of which we spoke in a previous chapter. The experience related by Gfeller can be observed by everyone. When we have looked for some time at an artistic painting so that our soul poured into the experience, we immediately afterwards see nature, a landscape, not only in a fresher and more colourful way, but we have come closer to it. After seeing a film, however, when we step into the open, nature appears to us paler, benumbed, more grey than usual. We have become estranged from her. Through looking at a painting our eye experiences enrichment of the life forces. The film we saw was possibly very interesting as regards its content, but it steals something of the pulsating life in my eye. The film somewhat dries up my process of seeing and even attacks my sense of own movement. This happens due to the unnatural technique that creates the illusion of movements of something that has been filmed. And it is even more true for images on a television screen.

Up to now we have only considered the eye. This is because within the whole sense organism it is the dominant organ. However, the other three senses do not function in an empty manner. Let us look at the sense of warmth. We speak of cold and warm colours. Is this a mere metaphor, a mere play on words? Underlying such an expression there is a reality. This refers us to hidden effects of colours. The blue wafts coolness to us, and vermilion radiates heat. We easily feel chilled in a room painted in a cold blue and we do not feel like shivering in a room of the same temperature painted in a warm red. Both, coolness and warmth which are not measurable with a thermometer, are perceived with our sense of warmth. This perception, although still of a sensory nature, already takes place at the border of the soul. There, the already metamorphosed, ensouled sense of warmth is active.

Is it possible for the sense processes of smelling and tasting to perceive the same stimulus through the artistic medium of colour? At first this does not seem to be the case. But there have been painters at all times who said that they also tasted the colours. By this they naturally did not mean tasting in the external sense. Barlach wrote in a letter of 1884: 'I paint on my walks, I taste, see and feel colour, the world is for me nothing but a host of colour spots.' From spiritual investigation Steiner answers two questions concerning the effect of colour on the sense organization. The one question, what connection exists between the colours and the middle sense organs, especially the processes of tasting and smelling; and the other question, is there a difference in the effect upon the sense processes, between colours which are inherent in nature, and the colours which we meet in a painting?

A certain leading back to the enlivening of
the senses takes place in the changes which
the artist undertakes with what is there to
hand ... And this is the reason that the artistic
perception is never aimed at such particular
sense spheres as the ordinary earthly perception.
The individual senses also enter into certain
relationships to one another, especially ... in
painting. In painting a remarkable symbiosis, a
remarkable functioning together of these sense
spheres takes place; not only in the coarser
organs, but in the broadening of the organs.
The painter or someone enjoying looking at
paintings does not only look at the colour,
the red, blue or violet, but in reality he tastes
the colours, only not with the coarse organs.
However, with everything around the realm
of the tongue, something is happening which
in a way is similar to the process of tasting. If
you simply look at a green parrot, you see with
your eyes the greenness of the colour. But if
you enjoy a painting, a fine, imaginative process
takes place in what lies behind the tongue, still
belonging to the tongue's sense of taste, and
partakes in the process of seeing. There are
similar fine processes to those when you taste
and take in food. It is not what happens on the
tongue, but the refined physiological processes
subsequently taking place that simultaneously
mingle with the process of seeing, so that the
painter on a deeper level actually tastes the
colour. And the nuances of colour he smells,
not with his nose, but with what takes place
in the organism with the act of smelling in

a deeper, more soul-like manner. In this way such combinations of the sense realms take place in that they move more into the spheres of the life processes.[14]

Through everything that up to now has been quoted about the being and effect of colours, the great educational value of the painting lesson in school becomes obvious. What is right for the adult holds good in a greater measure for the child, whose sense organism is far more receptive to all sense impressions. The group of the middle senses becomes ennobled through the medium of colour. With painting an important tool is given to the teacher.

4.5 Cultivating the cognitive senses

With the help of their four cognitive senses the children can learn to think and to understand the world. Everything connected with traditional learning through ideas mostly turns to the upper senses. On the basis of the perceptions of these sense organs children, as well as adults, form their view of the world. The learning capacity of a child depends on whether this group of senses has woken up and can be engaged. They can, however, develop properly only on the basis of well developed will senses. These must be cultivated intensively before the seventh year and also later in school. So a good part of the basis for learning is provided for in the first seven years and is the responsibility of the parents.

Children can develop their higher senses solely through another human being, actually only through adults. The organism of the children's upper senses is developed according to how the adults behave in their surroundings, to the extent they have developed the truly human element in their character, in their speech, in speaking and thinking, and in their whole personality. The adults represent those worlds of experience in which children exercise their cognitive senses. The adults, before all others, are the parents at home and the teachers in school. The children are forced for at least four hours, if not longer, to listen to the teacher. What an encroachment on their freedom! This is justified, even necessary, if it happens for the benefit of the children. The word 'listening' includes almost everything that belongs to the realm of the upper senses: sound, speech, thought and I. From what has been said up to now, it is clear that the cultivation of the children's cognitive senses constantly calls upon the educator's self-education. He is to educate in himself the four expressions of true humanity – his voice, speech, thought and sense for the I – so that he is worthy of the children's perception and imitation of these senses.

The sense of sound

We could say the voice of the teacher should sound entirely human. Every deviation from it goes in the direction of what is outside the human realm, the animal-like, even if only barely perceptible. We all know how easily a voice can be mixed with a gentle growl, a bleating, a grumble, a bark, a rattle. It is important to observe such tendencies and to eliminate them from one's voice. Every deep growl, every high falsetto are caricatures of the human voice. Children fashion their own voices in a human way with the help of the sense of sound which is one of the cognitive senses. With this sense organ children get to know a great deal about the good or bad habits of the teacher as soon as he begins to speak. The voice of the teacher tells them more about his character than the form of his nose, the expression of his face, his height, colour of his hair or eyes, and so on. Children can feel drawn to a teacher or feel repulsed by the tone of his voice. Some statements by Steiner may characterize this from an unfamiliar aspect.

> Man always has an intimate contact with his surroundings, especially with human surroundings … Two people sit facing each other, the one speaks, the other listens. Usually we believe the listener is inactive. This is not the case … It is not noticeable to outer perception, but very clear for the inner life that with the one who only listens everything the other does, even the movements of the physical vocal chords are copied, and the listener joins in speaking what the other one says. Everything you listen to, you speak with a faint movement of the vocal chords and of the speech apparatus which comes into play when speaking. And there is a considerable difference if the one who speaks possesses a croaking voice and you have to copy the corresponding movements or if he possesses a pleasant voice. In this respect the human being participates with everything and since this constantly happens it greatly influences the whole development of man.[15]

That everything of a musical nature serves the development of the sense of sound is so obvious that it does not require any further explanation. But let us remember that when we experience not just a single sound but also a musical work of art, the will senses, especially the sense of movement and of balance, take part too. We could never perceive and experience something of a real musical nature in any other way.

A question of great importance can confront us out of such connections as are here described. What happens to the formation of sound when the human voice and music are reproduced mechanically or electronically? It is not possible to give a generally valid answer. But I should like to close this section with an appeal from Edwin Fischer, a well-known musician whose word carried weight.

> You must learn to hear and to teach others to hear the difference which exists between an electrical sound distorted by a loudspeaker and a real, direct musical sound, as, for example, produced by a human voice or a cello.[16]

The sense of language

At first the teacher affects the children either for good or bad simply through his personality but apart from this he also affects them mostly through the word. He should have an especially close connection with language. We know, however, that the word as such is endangered in two directions, because it is used as a means for certain ends. It has to serve me, to express my wishes and demands, as well as to communicate my mental pictures and thoughts to another human being. In this way the word loses its own value, and we lose our feeling that a reality lies in the sounds, the words themselves, the language as a whole, something which can be perceived through the sense of language. Because of language being used in lowly ways it has been taken out of the spiritual realm where it originates. Its divine origin is forgotten and unrecognized, and we experience language only as a means of communication in the physical world. A challenge for the teacher would therefore be to find the way back to the word, to the being of language and therewith to the realm from which it originates; he should form his speech in accordance with this.

With this one task another is intimately connected: the training of the sense of speech. Through anthroposophy we are introduced to the way the human being of the past experienced the very being of language. In experiencing the twelve signs of the zodiac, human beings recognized twelve consonants, and in the movements of the planets in the constellations, they experienced the vowels. The whole alphabet was for them the 'expression of the harmony of microcosmic and macrocosmic secrets'. Such indications by Steiner can be a stimulus for us today to approach more closely and in all modesty the essence of sounds, the character of language.

In order to get close to the specific being of language, we have from time to time to be able to loosen language from its usual connections. In our consciousness we must free it from working only in the service of our thought communications and our desires. Thus we are able to become more conscious of the being of language. We become aware of the fact that language is the art of all arts, the true archetypal art. Consequently its being can only be laid hold of with an artistic sense.

Many symptoms indicate to the educator and doctor that the sense of language shows signs of degeneration. Consequently a new branch of healing had to be created, that of anthroposophical speech therapy. The speech therapist is concerned with certain newly appearing phenomena of a pathological nature which can only be interpreted as a deterioration of a sense organ – a sense organ which remained unnoticed as long as it functioned normally. We are speaking here of the sense of language. Although the functioning of the related sense, that of hearing, might function normally, the term 'word deafness' applies to situations where one is unable to perceive words, sound or language. We quote from a report from the World Congress for Speech Therapy in Frankfurt, 1965:

> Cases of word deafness are not at all rare
> with perfectly healthy hearing. The person
> afflicted does not understand the words and
> his mother tongue appears to him as foreign
> ... This condition can be congenital from
> birth. Children cannot distinguish between
> words or sounds. They experience the words
> and sounds as if they were any indiscriminate
> noises ... Rhythm and accentuation too which
> belongs to every language is not perceived by
> these children ... If word deaf children finally
> do learn to speak, but very late, they develop
> their own language, which only the family
> understands.[17]

Another report regarding the same problem showed that many people when they get old become hard of hearing. Hand in hand with this physiologically based lack of hearing there also appears a diminishing of understanding language, the cause of which is not properly known as yet. But it can often be observed that a person who still has comparatively good hearing has difficulty in following the spoken word.

Observations of this kind point quite clearly to the fact that the human being possesses a sense organ through which the language of a fellow human being can be perceived, an organ which by no means is identical with the organ of hearing. Since the sense of language is connected with the whole organism of movement and consequently also with the sense for our own movement, the attention of the speech therapist should be turned to such connections.

As soon as the sense of language opens up in young children, they begin to learn, through imitation, the language spoken around them. That the adults working with young children should speak a language suitable for training their sense of language is an educational challenge which concerns at first the parents, but later the teacher too. Children cannot learn to speak by themselves. It is known that feral children, children who for one reason or another lived in the wild before they learnt to speak, upon being found later could laugh and cry, but not speak.

The language of the teacher trains the language sense of schoolchildren in a direct way. It is therefore beneficial for them if the teacher has learned to pay attention to the character of his own language. Poetry is an enormous help in this as its mission is to endow the word with life and with soul. As stated earlier, poetry's true significance lies not in its conceptual content, but in the quality and pedagogical benefit of its sounds and rhythmic effect. The use of alliteration and various verse forms helps preserve the value of poetry.

Consequently with poetry, the teacher is given the means to cultivate the sense of language in the children. Let us remember what was said in the chapter concerning the cultivation of the will senses about the recitation and treatment of poems in the lessons. We can only indicate here that eurythmy is the most effective artistic medium to lead the sense of language to its higher goal.

The sense of thought

Let us first turn our attention not to the children, but to the teacher. His thoughts are perceived by the children. What about his thinking and his concept organism? He may think clearly, vaguely or even be confused. His thoughts may be true, half true or wrong, his concepts lively or barren and anaemic. His conceptual content may be rich or poor. His sense of thinking can be very active or lead a scanty existence. All this works on the children entrusted to him. It is precisely the upper senses which repeatedly challenge the educator to self-education.

However, schoolchildren up to their ninth or tenth year are not yet in a position to perceive thoughts in an abstractly conceptual form. Their sense of ideation has not yet reached this stage. We could call the preliminary stage of this sense organ the 'pictorial sense'. We have to acquaint ourselves with the thought that even the sense organs, especially the sense of thought and the sense for the I, experience a transformation in the individual development of the human being. Children before the ninth or tenth year can actually only perceive and understand such ideas and concepts which are given to them in the form of pictures. We find in all genuine myths, fairytales, fables, legends or religious documents, the classical way of giving thoughts and wisdom in pictures. With such thoughts saturated by pictures the children should be able, within a certain phase of development, to train their future sense of concept, hitherto active as a picture sense. This creates the best basis for a fully developed sense of thought appropriate for an adult.

Such facts of development make some demands on a lower school teacher. He has to be acquainted with the traditional world of fairytales and myths, which is rather a pleasant task to fulfil! Difficulties should only arise when thoughts and ideas, facts of all kinds have to be transformed into pictorial concepts in order to present them to children. The teacher will, however, experience every time he succeeds that the children readily accept it. The sense of thought developed in a lively way loves to perceive the same truth from various angles. It loves characterization. Its counterpart is the definition with which the schoolchild cannot deal at all. The teacher is not to practise definition, but characterization. Fairytales and myths can be his teachers. This can be shown with an example.

How can you convey to a seven- or eight-year-old what the human intellect is? How can young children, who have not developed the intellect, understand what this special capacity of the adult means? It is good that children perceive this power very early in a pictorial way. Their experience concerning the human being is to be enriched. This can take place through the two already mentioned methods of speaking in pictures and by characterizing. We often find characterization of the intellect in pictorial form in Grimm's Fairytales. The Brave Little Tailor is an intellectual madcap, not particularly likeable. Tom Thumb is preferable, but also an intellectual character. And Clever Elsa is a being who consists entirely of reason, and consequently can no longer act, and who in the end does not even know whether she inhabits reality or not.

Then there is the wretched story of Reynard the Fox who, with his intellectual cunning, cheats everybody but in the end has to live entirely isolated, outside human and animal society. In another fairytale the fox is torn apart by dogs in spite of his cunning. His 'intellect' has failed! Whoever is able to look aright through the pictorial and symbolic power of fairytales, will discover that in them the human intelligence is represented as a most valuable human faculty which can be a tremendous help in difficult, even dangerous, life situations. Behind the image of the horse, which so often plays a rescuing role in fairytales, the human intelligence is concealed. Without even once using the word intelligence or intellect, solely through pictorial characterization, we enable children through their faculty for pictorial sense perception to perceive different sides and qualities of the human reason.

The young child's pictorial organ is subject to the law of transformation as it develops into the organ of perception of concepts. Education has to help in this process. The pupils develop their sense of thought first according to the thoughts of the teacher. But even if this teacher could totally master his own thinking processes, it would not suffice to develop the sense of thought of a young person in a proper way. And so the teachers of upper school classes have welcomed help from the spiritual heroes of the past, thinkers of previous centuries, such as Plato, Socrates, Thomas Aquinas, Herder, Goethe, Schiller, Nietzsche and others. To perceive the thoughts of these spiritual heroes strengthens the sense of thought. The thinking of the young person should only serve to understand the thoughts of other people perceived in this way. The more young people perceive with understanding the strong thoughts of gifted thinkers, the better for their conceptual senses, and the better too, for the formation of their own thoughts in the future.

The perception of other people's thoughts creates the capacity to one day become an original thinker. Judgment and opinion, and the development of truly independent thinking occur at a later stage than many might imagine. Here we are speaking of enabling upper school students to understand the thoughts of another, and to refrain from judgment. Steiner says:

> The young person should have the attitude
> that he has first to learn ... Thinking before
> the eighteenth year should only serve to lay
> hold of what has been perceived, as it appears
> without the still unripe judgment seizing upon
> it ... Matters for which a judgment obtained
> by active thinking is necessary, cannot really
> be known until a certain point in life that is
> between the age of eighteen and nineteen.[18]

The sense for the I

The sense for the I is that faculty with which the adult can perceive something of the I of another human being. This I, or individuality, is the true essence of the primal human being who existed before birth and will continue after death. It is not the product of physical ancestors but points to the spiritual reality of the human being as, in fact, his own ancestor so to speak. But what about the sense of I of a schoolchild? It is true, his I has been active from early childhood, otherwise he could not stand upright and learn to walk, speak and think. But this I is actually only 'born', that is, working entirely from within, creating full self-consciousness, round about the twentieth year. Then the human being comes of age, and is responsible for his deeds or omissions.

As the child does not fully experience himself as an I-endowed human being, something else must come into play so that the child can experience the 'I-ness' of adults. It is difficult to express exactly how and what the child thereby perceives, or to give it a name. But we can call it a sense of and for authority, and observe that this develops around the age of seven. This is not the way one adult experiences the I of another adult, nor should it be. This has to do with the child's true need to experience the rightful authority of an adult who is acting out of his own sense of I.

To some extent this sense for authority is the representative of the sense for the I though this is not quite accurate. The sense for authority and the sense for the I stand in a similar relationship as the seed to the fully-grown plant. As illustrated earlier, the senses metamorphose from a lower stage of development to a higher stage as the human being grows and matures. May the teacher be for the children in his care this natural, beloved model, working from his own authentic authority, and so providing a basis on which the children can develop, at the right time, their own sense of individuality and freedom.

However, as little as the teacher alone as a thinking being would suffice fully to develop the sense of thought of the pupils, just as little could the sense for the I of the children solely develop out of the individuality of the teacher, even if this individuality were an extremely strong one. As is the case with the cultivation of the sense of thought, the teacher receives help for the cultivation of the I-sense from all directions. Each time the picture of the human being is brought in the right way to the children that something of their true being can become evident, the higher senses, and foremost the sense of I, are called upon. And this germinating consciousness of self constantly looks out for what is human. The perceiving of the human being is their nourishment.

The teacher brings the highest image of the human being to young children in, for example, fairytales, fables, legends, most of the myths and later in the biographies of significant personalities. One of the most important tasks in teaching is to present humankind in ever-new ways in the classroom. Each human character that is portrayed to the children completes this picture of the human being. In teaching, bringing the children stories of heroes or notable historical personalities, describing what they have thought, spoken, done and suffered, awakens the sense for the I and all the remaining cognitive senses. The becoming aware of and sympathising with the destiny of significant personalities has an especially strong awakening power on the budding consciousness of self. In everything that the teacher presents, especially in the way in which he does it, his own individuality always shines through. This cannot be entirely separated: the child simultaneously perceives the hero of whom the teacher speaks and the individuality of the teacher himself.

Knowledge of the human being in all its highest aspects appeals to the upper senses, especially to the germinating sense for the I. It is clear that in such subjects as history, geography, language, anthropology, and so on, the human being stands in the centre. Every other subject too gives the possibility, at least for moments, to be a study of the human being. The more surprising a new picture of the human being appears to the children, from apparently remote connections, the stronger the effect. All these different perceptions of the human being can then unite and, as a living synthesis, lead to the ideal of the human being. The most important aim of education is that the young person upon leaving school is endowed with comprehensive and versatile concepts of the human being.

Young people become well developed in their sense organism through the educational practice indicated here. This applies especially to their cognitive senses, which enable them to perceive in the right way voice, word, thought and self of the other human being. Let us not forget that in any social life a future human society has to be founded directly on the cultivation of the cognitive senses, but that these sense organs can only develop in the right way if all the other senses, if the entire human sense organism, has found its right care through education and self-education.

Notes

Volume Nos. of books by Rudolf Steiner refer to the Collected Works (CW), or to the German Gesamtausgabe (GA).

1. Introduction

1   *Toward Imagination,* CW 169, lecture of June 20, 1916.
2   *Nature Spirits,* CW 102, lectures of May 16 and June 4, 1908.
3   For instance, *Goethe's Theory of Knowledge,* CW 2; *Truth and Knowledge,* CW 3; *Philosophy of Freedom,* CW 4.
4   *From Crystals to Crocodiles,* CW 347, lecture of Sep 13 1922.
5   *The Foundations of Human Experience,* CW 293, lecture of Aug 29, 1919.
6   Goethe, *Maxims and Reflections,* No. 1061 & 295, and his poem, 'Vermächtnis'.
7   *Anthroposophy (A Fragment),* CW 45.
8   *The Renewal of Education,* CW 301, lecture of April 21, 1920.

2. The Human Sense Organism

1   *Anthroposophy (A Fragment),* CW 45.
2   *Rosicrucian Wisdom,* CW 99, lecture of May 31, 1907.
3   *The Riddle of Humanity,* CW 170, lecture of Sep 2, 1916.
4   *The Foundations of Human Experience,* CW 293, lecture of Aug 29, 1919.

5 *Anthroposophy (A Fragment)*, CW 45.
6 *The Philosophy of Freedom,* Addendum 1.
7 *The Riddle of Humanity,* CW 170, lecture of Sep 2, 1916.
8 *The Foundations of Human Experience,* CW 293, lecture of Aug 29, 1919.
9 *Anthroposophy (A Fragment),* CW 45.
10 *The Riddle of Humanity,* CW 170, lecture of Sep 2, 1916.
11 *Anthroposophy (A Fragment),* CW 45.
12 *The Riddle of Humanity,* CW 170, lecture of Sep 2, 1916.

3. The Development of the Sense Organism

1 *The Riddle of Humanity,* CW 170, lecture of Aug 12, 1916.
2 *The World of the Senses,* CW 134, lectures of Dec 28 & 29, 1911.
3 *Kunst und Lebensfragen,* GA 162, lecture of Aug 8 1915.
4 *The World of the Senses,* CW 134, lecture of Dec 29, 1911.
5 *Man as a Being of Sense and Perception,* CW 206, lecture of July 23, 1921.
6 *Man as a Being of Sense and Perception,* CW 206, lecture of July 23, 1921.
7 *Kunst und Lebensfragen,* GA 162, lecture of Aug 8, 1915.
8 This and the previous quote are from Steiner, *Die geistig-seelischen Grundkräfte der Erziehungskunst,* GA 305, lecture of Aug 19, 1922.
9 *True and False Paths in Spiritual Investigation,* CW 243, lecture of Aug 19, 1924.
10 *Heilfaktoren für den Sozialen Organismus,* GA 198, lecture of March 20, 1920.
11 *The Riddle of Humanity,* CW 170, lecture of Aug 15, 1916.
12 *Ancient Myths and the New Isis Mystery,* CW 180, lecture of Dec 26, 1917.
13 *The Riddle of Humanity,* CW 170, lecture of Aug 15, 1916.

4. Cultivating the Sense Organism Through Education

1 *Practical Advice to Teachers,* CW 294, lecture of Sep 1, 1919.
2 *Soul Economy,* CW 303, lecture of Jan 1, 1922.
3 Goethe, *Theory of Colours,* historical part.
4 Goethe, *Maxims and Reflections,* No. 664.
5 *Practical Advice to Teachers,* CW 294, lecture of Sep 1, 1919.
6 *Spiritual Science as a Foundation,* CW 199, lecture of Aug 8, 1920.
7 *Spiritual Science as a Foundation,* CW 199, lecture of Aug 8, 1920.
8 *Spiritual Science as a Foundation,* CW 199, lecture of Aug 8, 1920.
9 Kandinsky, *Point and Line to Plain.*
10 *Karmic Relationships,* Vol.2 , CW 236, lecture of April 27, 1924.
11 *The Riddle of Humanity,* CW 170, lecture of Aug 15, 1916.
12 *Soul Economy,* CW 303, lecture of Jan 3, 1922.
13 Simon Gfeller (1868–1943), *Vermächtnis, Aufzeichnungen aus seinem Tagebuch.*
14 *The Riddle of Humanity,* CW 170, lecture of Aug 15, 1916.
15 *The Being of Man and his Future Evolution,* CW 107, lecture of Dec 8, 1908.
16 Edwin Fischer (1886–1960) was a Swiss pianist and conductor. From the opening speech at his master classes in Lucerne.
17 *Frankfurter Allgemeine Zeitung* of Oct 27, 1965.
18 *The Education of the Child ,* (part of CW 34).

Bibliography

Gfeller, Simon, *Vermächtnis, Aufzeichnungen aus seinem Tagebuch,* (ed. Karl Uetz) Berne 1948.

Kandinsky, *Point and Line to Plain,* Dover, New York 1926.

Lauer, Hans Erhard, *Die zwölf Sinne des Menschen,* Novalis, Schaffhausen 1977.

Steiner, Rudolf. Volume Nos refer to the Collected Works (CW), or to the German Gesamtausgabe (GA).

—, *Ancient Myths and the New Isis Mystery* (CW 180) Anthroposophic Press, USA 1994.

—, *Anthroposophy (A Fragment): A New Foundation for the Study of Human Nature* (CW 45) Anthroposophic Press, USA 1996.

—, *The Being of Man and his Future Evolution* (CW 107) Rudolf Steiner Press, UK 1981.

—, *The Education of the Child ,* (part of CW 34) Anthroposophic Press, USA 1996.

—, *The Foundations of Human Experience* (CW 293) Anthroposophic Press, USA 1996.

—, *From Crystals to Crocodiles* (CW 347) Rudolf Steiner Press, UK 2002.

—, *Die geistig-seelischen Grundkräfte der Erziehungskunst* (GA 305) Dornach 1991.

—, *Goethe's Theory of Knowledge* (CW 2) SteinerBooks, USA 2008.

—, *Heilfaktoren für den Sozialen Organismus* (GA 198) Dornach 1984.

—, *Intuitive Thinking as a Spiritual Path,* Anthroposophic Press, USA 1995 (also published as *The Philosophy of Freedom).*

—, *Karmic Relationships,* Vol. 2 (CW 236) Rudolf Steiner Press, UK 1997.

—, *Kunst und Lebensfragen im Lichte der Geisteswissenschaft* (GA 162) Dornach 2000.

—, *Man as a Being of Sense and Perception* (CW 206) Steiner Book Centre, North Vancouver 1981.

—, *Nature Spirits* (CW 102) Rudolf Steiner Press, UK 2003.

—, *Philosophy of Freedom* (CW 4) Rudolf Steiner Press, UK 2012 (also published as *Intuitive Thinking as a Spiritual Path).*

—, *Practical Advice to Teachers* (CW 294) Anthroposophic Press, USA 2000.

—, *The Renewal of Education through the Science of the Spirit* (CW 301) Steiner Schools Fellowship, UK 1981.

—, *The Riddle of Humanity: The Spiritual Background of Human History* (CW 170) Rudolf Steiner Press, UK 1990.

—, *Rosicrucian Wisdom: An Introduction* (CW 99) Rudolf Steiner Press, UK 2000.

—, *Soul Economy: Body, Soul and Spirit in Waldorf Education* (CW 303) Anthroposophic Press, USA 2003.

—, *Spiritual Science as a Foundation for Social Forms* (CW 199) Anthroposophic Press, USA 1984.

—, *Toward Imagination: Culture and the Individual* (CW 169) Anthroposophic Press, USA 1990.

—, *True and False Paths in Spiritual Investigation* (CW 243) Anthroposophic Press, USA 1985.

—, *Truth and Knowledge* (CW 3) SteinerBooks, USA 2007.

—, *The World of the Senses and the World of the Spirit* (CW 134) Steiner Book Centre, North Vancouver 1979.

Index

life, sense of 29f, 57f, 69, 100,
  116
listening 123f

machine 104
Martin Luther 93
mathematics 32, 66f, 114
Melanchthon, Philipp 93
metabolic-limb human
  being 23
misperception 20–22, 47
modelling 111
Moon, Old 61
movement,
—, outer 34
—, sense of own 33–35, 56f,
  69, 101
music 113
myths 130

nerve-sense human being
  see sense-nerve human being

orientation, sense of (see
  balance, sense of)

painting 120f
perception 16–19, 20f, 72–76
—, cultivation of 86
physics 94
poetry 113f
Ptolemaic world view 92

rhythm 106f
rhythmic human being 23

sense impressions
—, nourishment of 15

sense-nerve human being 23
sight, sense of 38
skipping 105
sleeping 24
smell, sense of 40f, 117
sound, sense of 44–46, 123f
speech, sense of see language,
  sense of
speech therapy 127
spices 117
Steiner, Rudolf 13, 15, 26, 28,
  31, 49f, 52f, 56, 58, 65, 70f,
  77, 81f, 84, 97, 101, 112, 114
sympathy 54

taste, sense of 40f, 116
technology 78–80
thinking 72, 74–76
—, cultivation of 99
thought, sense of 44, 49, 57f,
  129f
touch, sense of 32f, 57f, 69,
  102f
Troxler, Ignaz 71

waking 24
warmth, sense of 21f, 37f, 40,
  42, 118
western culture 66, 68
will senses 28, 56
—, cultivation of 100
word
— deafness 127
—, sense of (see language,
  sense of)

More books for Steiner Waldorf Educators

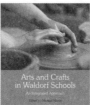

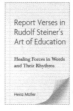

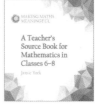